multiplanting

A Vision for Growing Churches,
Leaders and Mission

COLIN BARON
with Tom O'Toole and Tim Simmonds

malcolm down

PUBLISHING

Dedication

It is often said that books are a team effort. This one definitely is. So I'd like to dedicate *Multiplanting* to the magnificent people of Christ Church Manchester who have lived out the contents of this book with faithfulness, generosity and a sense of humour.

I am also grateful to the following people for their help with bringing this book to life:

Jennie Pollock and Andy Wisdom for their reading and editing skills.

Ian Watson for designing diagrams.

Liam Thatcher for advice and feedback.

Mike Knight, Tim and Aimee Windsor Brown, for reading various drafts.

This book is published in the 40th year of my ministry and more importantly the 40th year of marriage to Mary, which has proved to be the best decision I have made.

Really, this whole book is for Jesus who saved me as a wayward teenager and set me on a different path.

Colin Baron

Contents

Foreword
by David Devenish

I have had the pleasure of knowing and working with Colin Baron now for over 30 years. As well as Colin being one of my closest friends in ministry, I have learned over the years to admire his clarity of vision for the priority of church planting, both as an end in itself, and as a way of training leaders and thus fulfilling the Biblical mandate to make disciples. I have also grown to respect his wisdom and remarkable prophetic insight into issues affecting Christian leadership and his ability to get to the heart of both opportunities and problems that we are encountering. My own ministry has benefitted on numerous occasions from Colin's insightful remarks and his encouragement and frequent challenges to my own thinking in relation to my ministry in serving churches.

I am so glad that Colin has now decided to commit his insights into writing and the result is this excellent book *Multiplanting*. In it, these two particular qualities of Colin's ministry, vision for church planting and leadership wisdom, are combined to provoke much thought, prayer, inspiration and challenges to the traditional ways of doing ministry.

We need many more new churches and community based "sites" to be planted to reach this nation and other nations with the gospel. I therefore enthusiastically commend *Multiplanting* to you.

David Devenish – Team Leader, Newfrontiers Together Team.

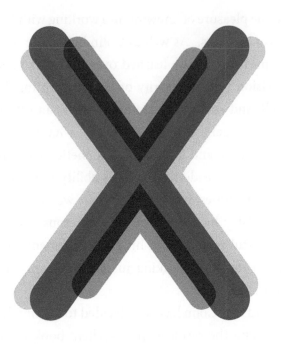

Part One:
Multiplanting and the
Big Church Dream

A few years ago, one of the leaders on my team told me of a time when he was walking with his father, who is an apple farmer, along a path through one of his orchards. The path divided the orchard into two parts: In one section there were lots of very large apple trees, between fifteen and twenty feet tall with a twenty-four-foot span. My friend noticed that because the trees were so big, they had to be spaced quite far apart.

On the other side of the path were smaller apple trees, about a third of the size of the larger ones, but there were many more of them. My friend became curious and wanted to know why there was such a difference between the two sections of the orchard. He was told that in the past, the general consensus in the apple farming industry had been that the best way to get more apples was to plant big trees far apart, because big trees produce more fruit than small trees. However, in the 1990s this thinking changed as apple farmers began to realise that the best way to get the most apples was not to plant a few big trees far apart but instead to plant lots of smaller trees close together. Each tree on its own produced less fruit than a large one could, but in the space that was required for one large tree, up to eight small trees could grow, and together they produced way more fruit than a single large tree.

Not only was the total apple yield larger, the apples from the smaller trees were of a far higher quality than those grown on the big trees, and apples became easier to harvest as ladders were no longer needed. Hundreds more trees could be planted, and they could be planted right to the edge of the field and in all the awkward corners that were impossible for the big trees to reach.

I believe that a time is coming when church leaders will have a similar mindset shift to the one experienced by those apple farmers. Many church leaders assume that the most effective path to fruitful kingdom ministry is growing a large church, but what if this big church dream is actually inhibiting us from seeing the quantity and quality of impact that we long for?

Over the last twenty-five years of ministry in Manchester, I have been pioneering a different approach; planting smaller, interconnected congregations throughout the city that operate together as one church. Strong enough together for each to survive and thrive, and yet small and dispersed enough to have a kind of reach that I would never have been able to have had I stayed in one place and grown big. I have called this approach 'multiplanting'.

Chapter One:
My Multiplanting
Journey

Have you ever found yourself in a car, having a conversation with your stereo as if it were a real person? I have.

It was 1993, and I was on my way to Manchester to have coffee with a couple of people whom I had never met before. They were friends of friends who had agreed to meet up with me and help me get to know the city a bit. A few months earlier, my wife Mary and I had sensed God calling us to move our family north and plant a new church somewhere in Greater Manchester. On the journey I was listening to a message from a Vineyard pastor named Steve Nicholson, who was challenging his congregation to dream again. He said that people had lost the courage to dream big dreams, and I strangely found myself responding to him as though he was in the car. 'My dream,' I said, 'is to plant twenty churches in Manchester.' It was at this moment that a multiplanting dream was birthed within me.

What is Multiplanting?

Multiplanting is a hybrid way of building church that draws on the strengths of many different approaches. I have seen lots of my friends plant and lead thriving churches using a wide variety of different models, and I wanted to incorporate as many of the positives as I could from these different approaches into my own ministry.

Big Churches or Small Churches?

Big churches have a lot going for them: By bringing a large number of people together, they have the resources to put on a comprehensive and varied ministry programme, the capacity to maximise the reach of their activities and the scale to have a genuine impact on a whole city or region.

Small churches also have a lot of advantages: It is much easier to foster a community feel in a smaller church, and there are opportunities for people to get involved quickly, and be entrusted with ministry responsibility that they would be unlikely to receive in a larger church.

Before coming to Manchester I had been involved in two church plants, and neither of them had been a roaring success! The first plant was in Buckinghamshire, and I naïvely thought that because we were a group of very motivated and talented people, as well as good friends, new people would flock to us in droves! Although we all worked hard and the fellowship was wonderful, growth was slow and not as I expected. The second church plant was in a very needy area of North Kent, planting with a much smaller team (albeit still of excellent people). In light of my previous experience, the smaller team and the much poorer community that I was planting into, I had much lower expectations this time around, and my main strategy was based around simply surviving. Not exactly an inspiring vision for the future!

Again, the team worked wholeheartedly, but it took several years before we succeeded in building a small – but growing – church. We then made the 250-mile journey north to start again in Greater Manchester. After the challenges of the first two plants, I was determined to come up with a strategic plan to build a church that would see many people saved, God's kingdom breaking in and creation being restored. Like many church leaders, I was keen to build something of size and capacity. Although I don't like to admit it, numbers really mattered to me, and the fact that I had been unable to build anything with more than eighty members hurt. Over time, I realised that I was in the same boat as the overwhelming majority of church leaders in the West. Recent research from the Evangelical Alliance shows that the average congregation size of churches in the UK is eighty-four (the figure for the USA is similar),[1] and most of the leaders of these churches are desperate to see their churches grow, but have little idea how to get some momentum going.

As I began dreaming of planting in Manchester, I couldn't get away from the dream that I first vocalised during that car journey when I was listening to Steve Nicholson's message. I didn't just want to plant one church; I wanted to plant twenty! This led me to reset the parameters of how I saw myself and how I would build church. Instead of struggling against the eighty-member ceiling, I began to embrace it. I realised that I could look at Greater Manchester through the lens of not just a single church, but of multiple church plants. If I could get twenty churches started and they each grew to fifty, then that would be a thousand people. This felt to me much more achievable than gathering a thousand people in a single congregation.

If we could bring together a thousand people, we would be able to enjoy the benefits of big churches, with the resources and capacity to serve people in a wide variety of ways, and make a splash in the city. But by doing so as congregations of between fifty and eighty members, we would be able to tap into the advantages of smaller churches, creating communities where people could feel known, loved and at home, and given lots of opportunities to step up and have a go at using their gifts. Our multiplanting approach meant that we were able to get the best of both worlds.

City Churches or Community Churches?

City churches are churches that have a vision to reach a whole city. They are ambitious and bold, often located near the centre of a city, and they aim to gather people in from all across a city on a Sunday and then see those people influence their own communities in the week. City churches can often be influential and exciting. They have a lot going for them.

Community churches are also very exciting, though their form is very different to city churches. The idea is for a church to go deep within one particular community. This may be a village or small town, or may be a specific local area within a larger city. They can form strong relationships with people, businesses and organisations that are part of that community, and become a loved and respected part of community life.

Not too long after I arrived in Manchester, I was invited to attend a conference hosted by a church in Sale. A prophet named Bryn Franklin got up to speak, and he pointed to me and a friend who was sitting next to me. Bryn had never met us before, and knew nothing about us, but he spoke to my friend and described part of a conversation that we had had that afternoon, and even gave us the answer to the questions that we had been asking. I was amazed! He said to me, 'I don't know you, but you are a leader and you are a large stake in the ground firmly driven in. Around you I see lots of stakes and they are all webbed together.'

I knew this was part of the answer to how we build the twenty churches that I had been dreaming of. A web is strong and flexible. It is interlinked and has purpose. If we were to start a movement of churches, they could be linked together and provide strength, resources and support that no individual church could muster up on its own. Each of the stakes could engage deeply in its own local community, and yet through the web that formed we could also have city-wide impact.

Very quickly, we started churches in Bolton, Warrington, Oldham, Salford, Stockport and Macclesfield. Our approach was simple: we found a few people to get it started and then we commissioned them to gather and grow. The strength and flexibility of the web was key as it gave us lots of room to initiate new plants whilst still experiencing the security and fellowship of the whole. It also meant that rather than taking resource out of the centre, each new plant actually strengthened the whole. Both our city impact and local engagement increased with every new plant that we started. We were able to benefit from both the breadth of vision that is usually associated with a city church and the depth of vision that comes from a community church. Once again, our multiplanting approach meant that we were able to get the best of both worlds.

Church Planting or Multisite?

Church planting is adventurous and entrepreneurial. This pioneering endeavour creates an environment of faith, provides opportunities for new young leaders to step out and has been shown to result in tremendous kingdom growth.

Multisite is another way of expanding church into new areas. It offers more resources and stability than church planting, but also can reduce both the need for innovation and the opportunity for new people to step up and pioneer a way.

I have always been aware that pioneering is part of the ministry that God called me to, and I remember that as a young man at Bible college, I felt particularly stirred when I heard people talking about pioneering missionary work. My calling as a pioneer was confirmed when, in the first church I planted, my friend Terry Virgo came to appoint me as an elder in the church. Terry travelled to us with some prophets, and during the evening, prophetic words were given about me being a pioneer. As Terry got up to speak, he started by sharing that he thought that God had told him earlier in the day that he must change the talk from his usual eldership sermon to one about Joshua pioneering into the Promised Land. It was only when he had heard those prophetic words that he understood why God had given him that instruction. We had thought the evening would be all about 'praying in' a pastor, but in fact it felt more like commissioning a pioneer!

When I arrived in Manchester, and felt stirred by the dream of starting twenty churches and the picture I had been given of the stakes and the web, we quite quickly got a few congregations planted around Manchester that operated as a network together. These congregations were held together by common values, shared finances, and everybody celebrating what we were as a whole (including how many of us there were!). We made sure that all of the site leaders spent some of their time working on their site and other time helping another part of the larger church. We worked hard to find appropriate ways to express our togetherness. One of the most significant things we did together was to hold nights of prayer three times a year. These were amazing gatherings where different worship bands and prophetic leaders would take sessions. We would worship our God together, intercede, eat food at midnight and share great camaraderie, in the knowledge that we were on an amazing journey together.

By the time we had started our eighth congregation in Tameside it was becoming clear that we needed to define more precisely what we were doing. Were we building one church that happened to have multiple congregations (which would today be known as a multisite church) or were we planting lots of churches that happened to be networked together? This was a difficult time for me personally, as I felt way more invested in the whole than in any one congregation, yet the trajectory that had been set was that we would move to each congregation being independent and self-governing. Having set this initial objective, it became clear in time that each of the congregations did need to forge its own identity. This, plus a door opening for my family to spend two years ministering in the north-eastern seaboard of the USA, eventually brought an end to the multicongregation and the start of a new season for everybody. Of the eight churches that we had planted, six have prospered and one has planted again. The other two folded, sadly, despite having experienced seasons of good growth.

My reflection on this first phase of planting in Manchester was mainly very positive. We had managed to get growth into the hundreds, with leaders who probably wouldn't have done so well on their own. It also helped me to realise how important the trajectory that you set from the start is for how things develop and grow. For example, you may have noticed that, as I have told the story so far, I have called the gatherings that we were planting 'congregations'. In those early days, we were not sure what terminology would be best to use, but because church planting was the goal, we felt that language that pointed in this direction (without going as far as explicitly calling them 'churches') was important, and so we settled on the term 'congregations'.

Looking back, I can see that setting this trajectory and choosing this language ended up bringing to an end, probably earlier than would have been beneficial for some, our corporate journey and the sharing of resources that was possible when we operated as a single multicongregation church. This was definitely the case in one of the churches that closed, and also in the case of the last church that we started, late on in the journey. This church failed to gain traction in numerical growth when it was no longer a part of the whole. It was in this last of the churches, now called Christ Church Manchester (CCM), that the second phase of my ministry in Manchester began.

When we returned from the USA in 2006 we were invited to join this church, and I can honestly say that it was quite an emotional journey for the first few years. I loved America, and though we had known that we would only be there for a short time, I found it hard to adjust to being back; it was particularly hard to start again with just one location as I had so loved the buzz and vibe that had come with being part of something much bigger, both in the States and in my first spell in Manchester.

Building on the past, and having learned some important lessons from what happened the first time around, we now wanted to set a new trajectory that would maintain a much longer-term unity. One of the first decisions that we made was to start thinking in terms of 'sites' rather than 'congregations'. We still wanted to keep a pioneering edge and to plant into new areas from scratch, rather than just hiving off subsets of our existing congregation, and we still wanted local leaders to be able to take leadership responsibility in their site and figure out how to reach their community in meaningful ways. Nevertheless, we felt that building something that would stay together as one church across all of these sites was the right trajectory for us, and so the strategic choices that we made and the language that we employed were all geared in this direction.

The other helpful ingredient was the geography that we covered. In the first phase, the congregations that we had planted covered an area of over forty miles, so it was understandable that they wanted to cultivate their own identity to reach the town or community in which they were based. In this new phase, however, our sites were much more tightly concentrated near the centre of Manchester. This has helped us to build unity in the church and create a feeling of shared ownership of the mission.

I mentioned earlier the prophetic word that I had been given just after I arrived in Manchester about the stakes that would be webbed together. Each of our sites is one of those stakes, but by keeping the connection and oneness between them, we find that the whole is both stronger and more flexible than the individual stakes could be on their own. Working this way means that a creative tension needs to be maintained. Each of the stakes needs to have its own strength, and a lot of my time is spent working with our site leaders, providing support and coaching, and I find myself getting involved in whichever sites could most benefit from my strengthening input. At the same time, we also need each site to appreciate the value of the whole and work hard on unity. I have found that when site leaders can only see a vision for their own site, they tend to struggle, but when site leaders lift their heads and engage with the bigger picture, this has brought strength both to the whole church and to the individual site that they lead.

In this second phase, we switched trajectories from something that would move towards independence to something that would maintain unity. In this sense, we could be described as multisite, but we are probably not what most people think of when they hear the phrase 'multisite church'. At our heart we are still pioneers, and in the ten years that we have been on this journey with CCM we have planted five sites, with six meetings every Sunday. We are intending to plant many more, and we have developed a way of doing so that has been described as 'lean and scalable'. We will talk about this more as the book goes on.

We have identified some important things that we believe need to be centrally owned (the name, the vision and culture, the eldership, the finances, and certain celebration events such as baptisms) and we work hard from the centre to communicate well and make life easy for people on the ground. Outside of these things, however, we try to devolve as much to the site level as possible. All our preaching and worship music is organised by the individual sites, and each site is empowered to develop whatever programming best serves its mission to reach its own community.

By continuing to pioneer, we have created the faith environment that comes with church planting, built a momentum that snowballs with every new plant, and made genuine space for young leaders to have a go and make a difference. At the same time, we have also found the strength, flexibility and unity that comes from a commitment to remain together as one group. Once again, our multiplanting approach means that we are able to get the best of both worlds.

At the time of writing, Christ Church Manchester currently has sites in Gorton, Fallowfield (two Sunday meetings), Withington, Burnage and our most recent plant into Manchester city centre. We also have people in a few different areas of the city starting to pray, gather and dream about what could be next for us. Altogether there are around 300 people in CCM, plus around 500 in the previous multicongregation that we planted. The original dream of getting twenty churches started, and reaching a thousand people fifty to eighty at a time, is not very far way at all. And the journey is only just beginning.

Chapter Two:
The Call to Pioneer

In his book, *The Tipping Point*,[2] Malcolm Gladwell explores the idea of Dunbar's Number, named after the anthropologist Robin Dunbar, who suggested that as communities grow there comes a point 'beyond which members of any social group lose their ability to function effectively in social relationships'. Dunbar suggests this number is 150, but he also observes other thresholds at which the quality of community is diluted: particularly when that community reaches five, ten and fifty members.

The more time I spend engaging with church leaders, the more I think Dunbar's work applies. Lots of churches get stuck and struggle to break fifty, and many more struggle to break 150. Significant structural changes are needed to cross these thresholds and it naturally comes at a cost to the quality of community when a church grows from a place where everybody knows one another, to one where they don't.

Having to choose between growth and community can feel like an impossible choice, because both are fundamental to the kingdom of God and his church. And yet there is a biblical pattern which shows us that we can indeed grow the kingdom, and do so in a way that is built around vibrant and healthy communities. Rather than planting one large church in the centre of a city or region, and expecting everybody to travel in to your meeting place, instead start lots of mutually supporting smaller churches (or sites or congregations – call them what you will) into all the different communities of your city or region. This is both an effective way of reaching every part of a city or region with the gospel, and a model that ensures that everybody has access to a close-knit community of friends that correlates with Dunbar's research. It is also an approach to ministry that matches the New Testament example of Jesus himself and his first apostles.

Jesus was a Pioneer

In the early days of Jesus' public ministry, we see him begin to train his disciples and to set forth the pattern that those same disciples would adopt as they went on to preach the gospel and start churches. In Mark 1, we find both a biblical model for ministry and an insight into the priorities that occupied Jesus as he gathered his fledgling community. After an initial season of preparation through the ministry of John the Baptist, and Jesus' own baptism and temptation, the gathering began (verse 14). Jesus (on his own) went into an area and began preaching the gospel in that place. He quickly gathered a core team, and they went about evangelising and teaching. It wasn't long before word got out and a crowd started to form. This is the kind of opportunity that, as church leaders, we long for. People are responding to Jesus' ministry. New people are showing up. Lives are getting changed. Here is a chance to do something significant in Capernaum.

Rather than simply being swept along by events, Jesus got up very early the next morning and went to a desolate place to pray. After a frantic search for much of that day, Jesus' disciples finally managed to locate him, and Simon blurted out, 'Everyone is looking for you' (Mark 1:37). Simon was drawing Jesus' attention to the crowd of people that had gathered and the opportunity that had presented itself back in Capernaum. There were at least three compelling reasons for Jesus to go back and create a semi-permanent ministry base there:

- *There was big demand.* Lots of people there wanted a piece of Jesus. It is the kind of public attention that most of us crave for our churches to have in our local communities.

- *There were real needs.* We are told in Mark 1:34 that Jesus healed *many* who had diseases, in contrast to other places where he healed *every* disease (see, for example, Matthew 9:35). There were still people in Capernaum who needed healing, not to mention those who were yet to hear the good news of the gospel.

- *People were willing to travel.* Jesus was beginning to get a reputation and word about him was spreading through Galilee. Jesus could have set up a base of ministry in Capernaum and had people come to him from all around.

Under such circumstances, many of us would be tempted to stay put and make the most of the opportunity before us (in fact, we may well look for a way to increase the scope of what we were doing there to make the most the interest), but Jesus declined the opportunity and instead made the remarkable suggestion, 'Let us go on to the next towns, that I may preach there also, for that is what I came for' (Mark 1:38). Instead of remaining in Capernaum and taking advantage of this ministry opportunity,

Jesus led his disciples through the different towns and villages of Galilee, preaching in the synagogues and casting out demons.

Though there were compelling reasons for staying where he was, Jesus knew that the arguments for going to the next places were better:

- *The call of God.* Immediately before Jesus' decision to leave Capernaum and go on tour, he had risen early and found a quiet place to pray. Through his times with the Father, Jesus maintained a crystal clarity about what God was calling him to do. It is as we spend time with the Father and are refocussed on our callings that we are able to make radical pioneering decisions, even when there is pressure to remain and build where we are.

- *Training the disciples.* Had Jesus remained, it would have been easy for the disciples to think that they had already achieved success by establishing a ministry in Capernaum and that their task now was simply to maintain that ministry. For most of the disciples (and indeed for Jesus at this point in his life), Capernaum was home. Jesus needed to raise their heads with an apostolic vision for all the nations of the earth. This mobility that Jesus built into his initial community was a big factor in enabling the gospel to spread so rapidly in the book of Acts.

- *The scope of the mission.* God's big mission is, and always has been, for his glory to spread across all of the earth. Within this, during the three-year ministry of Jesus, he was to go to 'the lost sheep of the house of Israel' (see Matt. 15:24). The scope of this mission was way bigger than a single town; and to reach every town and village would have been a challenging task, even more so had Jesus remained in Capernaum.

As attractive as it would have been to stay put in Capernaum and establish a regional base, it would have been, at best, a partial success. There would have no doubt been a thriving ministry established there, with regular healings, wonderful teaching and changed lives, but the impact of this ministry would have remained geographically constrained.

In many churches today, there is a Capernaum mindset. We (rightly) celebrate the good things that God is doing in our areas, and we dream, strategise and pray about how we can maximise these things. But in doing so, the danger is that we miss the bigger opportunity that is before us.

The Harvest is Plentiful...

A little while later in his ministry, Jesus was doing exactly what he had left Capernaum to do—ministering in the towns and villages—when something happened that led him to take his pioneering strategy to a whole new level.

And Jesus went throughout all the cities and villages, teaching in their synagogues and proclaiming the gospel of the kingdom and healing every disease and every affliction. When he saw the crowds, he had compassion for them, because they were harassed and helpless, like sheep without a shepherd. Then he said to his disciples, 'The harvest is plentiful, but the labourers are few; therefore pray earnestly to the Lord of the harvest to send out labourers into his harvest'. (Matthew 9:35–38)

As he thought about these people, Jesus knew two things: The first was that these crowds were repeated in every town and village across Israel (if not the world), and all of them desperately needed to be reached (and it wouldn't happen by sitting tight where he was and waiting for them to come to him). The second thing Jesus knew was that by going as one team of twelve, they would not be able to get to every town and village in the three years that were available to them.

The need today is no less than it was in Jesus' day, and the size of the task can feel equally overwhelming. As we cast our minds to the communities, towns and villages that surround our churches, not to mention the nations of the earth, our hearts too must be moved with compassion and desire to see those people meet with Jesus. But what can we do when the need is so great, and our capacity to reach those people barely scratches the surface of what is required? Jesus responded by doing two things: He asked for prayer about the situation, and he multiplied his pioneering ministry.

Prayer is crucial. Jesus knew that the harvest was out there, but he also knew that there was a chronic shortage of pioneers who could go and break open the land to yield its harvest. So he asked all of his disciples to pray for an increase in the number of workers that God would send into the field. This is a great thing to do as we are overwhelmed by the needs around us.

In my experience, prayer meetings are often the place where the pioneering breakthroughs happen. In the early days after moving to Manchester, inspired by the prophetic word I had been given about the stakes and the web, I had gathered around fifty people and we were praying for an increase in church planting in Greater Manchester. At this time, there was a young girl called Susan amongst our number, who lived twenty miles away in Bolton. One Friday evening as we were praying together as a church, I looked over to Susan and said to the gathering, 'Why don't we pray about the possibility of planting into Bolton?' I had said it in quite a half-hearted way, deliberately underplaying the idea out of a fear of failure and of sounding ridiculous (after all, there were only fifty of us in the church at this time), but as we were praying I sensed God challenge me with the question, 'Have I called you to plant twenty churches, or to be half-hearted about it?' I interrupted the meeting and explained what had just happened to me. That night we agreed together as a church that we were planting a church with Susan and her dog, and Bolton Family Church was born. That church is now around 120 people and has itself been active in church planting.

Prayer is vital. But prayer is not the only thing that Jesus did, and if our only response to the need around us is to pray, then at times it can become a hiding place that inoculates us from the part that God is asking us to play in his pioneer mission. As the narrative continues into Matthew 10, we see the second response that Jesus made to the needs around him: he multiplied his pioneering resources.

> And he called to him his twelve disciples and gave them authority over unclean spirits, to cast them out, and to heal every disease and every affliction. The names of the twelve apostles are these: first, Simon,

who is called Peter, and Andrew his brother; James the son of Zebedee, and John his brother; Philip and Bartholomew; Thomas and Matthew the tax collector; James the son of Alphaeus, and Thaddaeus; Simon the Cananaean, and Judas Iscariot, who betrayed him.

These twelve Jesus sent out, instructing them, 'Go nowhere among the Gentiles and enter no town of the Samaritans, but go rather to the lost sheep of the house of Israel. And proclaim as you go, saying, "The kingdom of heaven is at hand." Heal the sick, raise the dead, cleanse lepers, cast out demons.' (Matthew 10:1–8)

Even though many people had been healed, fed, taught and delivered from demons under Jesus' own ministry, there were so many more to get to that Jesus split his twelve apostles into pairs and sent them out to do the ministry that he had been doing. As a result, Jesus was able to multiply his ministry six-fold and have a much larger pioneering impact on the towns and villages of Israel. Despite this increase, this pioneering task was still too great, and so Jesus needed to multiply himself further, and in Luke 10, he sends out seventy-two others. Having initially moved from one ministry team to six, Jesus now gave himself another six-fold increase, with thirty-six teams now ministering in the different towns and villages.

Jesus' strategy in his ministry was a simple one: He wanted to get the good news to all the villages of Israel, and he knew that to do this he would need to go to them. Jesus was a pioneer who looked to get to people where they were at and preach the gospel to them, and to develop others who could do the same. Staying in one place and hoping that the impact would spread to the edges wasn't enough; Jesus wanted to multiply his ministry into every community he could.

The Apostolic Mission

This pioneering ministry of Jesus and his close followers served as perfect preparation for the mission that Jesus would give to his disciples after his death and resurrection. In the conversations that the risen Christ had with his followers, there are two key themes that come up over and over again. Both have to do with the mission that he had given them.

The first theme is the expanded *scope* of the mission. During the three years of Jesus' earthly ministry, the focus was on preaching the kingdom throughout Israel. In fact, Jesus explicitly says in Matthew 15:24 that, 'I was sent only to the lost sheep of the house of Israel'. This isn't to say that no Gentiles were blessed through his ministry, but the clear drive was to get to every town, village and community in Israel. Following his resurrection, Jesus widened the focus of the work from Israel to the whole world. In Luke 24:47 he explains that 'repentance and forgiveness of sins should be proclaimed in his name *to all nations*, beginning from Jerusalem' (emphasis added). The disciples were to do the things that he had shown them, but now with a focus on all nations of the earth.

The second theme that was repeatedly emphasised by the risen Christ was the new *power* for the mission. Though Christ would not be with them in person, he would send them the Holy Spirit who would empower them for the task. This promise of the Spirit was fulfilled on the day of Pentecost, and we immediately see a nod to the new global scope of the mission as the Spirit enabled the disciples to praise God in different languages, meaning that people from many nations could hear the good news of what God had done. As the book of Acts progresses, we see the disciples getting on with their mission, following the pattern that Jesus had set. They started in Jerusalem but, before long, persecution had scattered them. Wherever they went they preached Jesus, healed the sick and planted churches. The gospel reached Samaria and then Damascus, Caesarea and Antioch. The church in Antioch was planted by Greek-speaking believers from Cyprus and Cyrene, and it soon became a hub for church planting and pioneering into other parts of the Greek-speaking world. What had started with a great church in Jerusalem was now becoming a truly unstoppable movement. Not only is each church growing in its own right, but new churches are being started too that accelerate the growth dynamic. The commission was never just to build a big church, but to make disciples of the nations, and by the time we reach Antioch in Acts 11, this was starting to take place.

A few years after the Antioch church was started, the leaders of the church had gathered to worship and pray. The Holy Spirit spoke to them, instructing them to send out two of their team – the apostles Barnabas and Paul – as travelling missionaries and church planters. The strategy that Barnabas and Paul (and later Paul with Silas and Timothy) employed in their planting is fascinating. Rather than going to every town and village they could find, or even every city, they very deliberately honed in on the most prominent city in each region; and churches were started in places like Philippi, Corinth and Ephesus.

By the time Paul wrote his letter to the church in Rome, he claimed to have 'fulfilled the ministry of the gospel of Christ' (Rom. 15:19) in an area from Jerusalem all the way around to Illyricum. This was an area of around 1,400 miles and included the cities that he had planted into. What could he possibly mean when he says that he has fulfilled the ministry of the gospel in that area? Clearly, Paul did not preach the gospel to every single person who lived in that region, nor did he start a church in every town or village between Jerusalem and Illyricum (there would have been hundreds, if not thousands, of them to get to). Rather, by planting into the major cities of each region, Paul had the expectation that from each of these churches, the gospel would spread throughout a whole region.

When Paul left Titus in Crete, his instruction was to 'appoint elders in every town' (Titus 1:5). Though Paul himself had not been involved in planting into every town in Crete, the whole island had been reached because a multiplying, church planting movement had started there that could plant new churches in every town. The apostolic strategy for reaching the world with the gospel was to open up a new region and start a church there that could take responsibility for planting through that region and reaching every community in their area.

As I sat in my car twenty-five years ago, screaming at my stereo that 'my dream is to plant twenty churches', I believe that I was tapping into something profoundly biblical. The call to reach a region really ought to be part of the DNA of every church, and I constantly find myself both challenged and inspired by the scope of this apostolic vision. Over the last couple of decades, I have learned a lot about what it takes to spread churches throughout a region (and I am sure I still have much more to learn). In the rest of this book I will share some of the principles that have been key to our journey so far. Now, in my seventh decade of life, I am more passionate than ever about pioneering and doing whatever I can to help spread the church into as many towns, villages and communities as possible.

'Let us go on to the next towns... for that is what I came for' (Mark 1:38).

Chapter Three:
How Multiplanting
Works

When I think back on the two phases of my ministry in Manchester, the biggest change the second time around was the clarity that I had gained on what should be led from the centre and what should be devolved to the local sites. These questions around centralisation are crucial for pioneers to answer, and what you build will look radically different depending on how you approach this issue.

Some of the best thinking on the subject has been done by Brad House and Gregg Allison in their excellent book, *Multichurch*. In particular, in chapter 3 they present a very helpful analysis of seven different models of church that form a spectrum of centralisation for multisite churches to consider, as illustrated in their diagram below:[3]

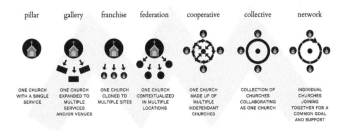

Source: Brad House and Gregg Allison, Multichurch (Grand Rapids, MI: Zondervan, 2017), p48

As the models move from left to right, they become increasingly decentralised, with more and more power and authority expressed locally.

The first model that they offer is the *Pillar* church, which would reject any idea of multisite and would instead be a single independent congregation, all gathering together for a single worship service.

Second, there is the *Gallery* model, which is the first of three models that House and Allison refer to as 'multisite'. In this model a church will multiply services within the same venue, either by having overflow rooms or repeat services at different times.

The third model, also multisite, is the *Franchise* model where a church will have multiple locations, but the experience is tightly managed to be the same at each site. This would include heavily centralised leadership and programming, and usually the same teaching at all sites, with a charismatic lead pastor being video streamed into every location.

The final third multisite model is *Federation*, which is 'one church that is contextualised in multiple locations'. Like the other multisite models, this would involve being one church with a central strategy, culture and approach, but where each site is genuinely empowered to find effective ways of reaching their local community, and determines and delivers teaching and music locally.

Next on the spectrum is *Cooperative*, which House and Allison describe as the first of two 'multichurch' models. Again there is a common vision and identity along with local contextualisation, but a much greater emphasis is given to local leadership in shaping the whole. This would be described as interdependent churches choosing to cooperate for a common goal.

The other 'multichurch' model described is a *Collective*, where the idea of 'interdependence' would be replaced with 'independence'.

There would be even less centralised leadership and the onus would very much be on the individual churches to buy in to the collective identity to the extent that it works for them.

Finally, there is the *Network* model, where churches are largely independent but choose to associate with each other in a kind of fellowship.

For a church that is thinking about what it would mean to reach a whole region whilst also engaging deeply in local communities, the five models at the centre of House and Allison's spectrum are worthy of consideration, providing different approaches that range from highly centralised to primarily localised. The model that House and Allison advocate for in their book is 'cooperative', and this is the model that most closely aligns to what I did in my first season of planting in Manchester. Having set a trajectory towards each church carrying authority locally and yet working together interdependently, I can appreciate a lot of strengths inherent in the model. It certainly fosters faster and healthier growth than many of the other approaches that I have observed.

Nevertheless, as I reflect back on this season of ministry, I am also very aware of the weaknesses present in this model. Specifically, I found that by decentralising some key areas around identity and vision, I lacked the levers that I required to maintain a clarity of purpose and cohesion. As each site embraced its own sense of identity and vision, we found that an element of diversion was inevitable, and the model of how the churches operated together began drifting further to the right of the spectrum. Whilst this is not necessarily a bad thing in and of itself, it had the effect of weakening the bonds of support between the churches and stalling further multiplication in the city.

In our second wave of planting in Manchester, we have been much more strategic about what is delegated locally and what is held centrally. We are passionate about empowering our local sites to contextualise and work out the mission in their own area, and equally passionate about holding together a united and city-wide approach. We have found the model that is described as 'federation' serves the purpose very well indeed, giving us a shared vision, culture, leadership, budget and identity. This allows plenty of space for localised programming, teaching, mission and community, and creating an environment where we can continue to pioneer new sites into new parts of the city.

Central and Local

I believe the key to making multiplanting work successfully is knowing what areas to hold centrally and what to devolve locally to the sites.

Below are outlined some examples of where I have found this to be most crucial. I will unpack these in greater detail as the book goes on.

Mission: Central Vision, Local Engagement

Jesus has given his church a mission: 'Go therefore and make disciples of all nations, baptising them in the name of the Father and of the Son and of the Holy Spirit, teaching them to observe all that I have commanded you' (Matthew 28:19-20). This mission is not up for discussion, and should be the cornerstone of the vision and mission of every Christian and every local church. In fact, I once heard Stef Liston helpfully suggest that the vision of a local church should be nothing more or less than 'a culturally relevant articulation of the Great Commission plus a concise way of expressing any promises God has made to you.'[4]

At Christ Church Manchester, this comes back to the dream I had of starting twenty churches when I was listening to Steve Nicholson in my car, and the prophetic picture of the stakes and web that God gave to back it up. The vision is to make disciples in Manchester and beyond by starting new interconnected churches throughout the city. This vision is one that is shared across Christ Church Manchester, and we have worked hard to ensure that leaders and members at each of our sites are working towards this vision as they engage in their local communities. I have at times had site leaders or community groups speak in terms of developing their own vision for their site or group, but I find it much more helpful to think in terms of finding their place within the overall vision than formulating a vision of their own (after all, the word 'division' literally means two visions, and Jesus himself taught that a house divided against itself cannot stand – Matt. 12:25).

The idea of finding a place within a vision is, I believe, a very useful one. There will always be some people who find the big picture inspiring and others who are much more motivated about the local application, and multiplanting creates space for both. For those who gravitate towards the city-wide advance and the next plant, there is lots of work to do and opportunity to get involved, whereas those who want nothing more than to put down deep roots and make disciples in a local community tend to be the pillars on which our sites are built and appreciate the resourcing and support that is offered them by the whole church.

Leadership: Central Authority, Local Empowerment

I am sometimes asked about the difference between multisite and church planting and, depending on the models used, the differences may be few or many. For me, the key way to define whether a plant is a site or a separate church is to look at where the authority lies – is it with local leaders in that congregation or with leaders who are responsible for a number of local sites or congregations?

At Christ Church Manchester, it is important to us that we are united in our mission in the city, and this means that we want there to be a commonality of leadership across our sites. It is also important to us that every site is part of this leadership. It would not be healthy to ask local leaders to submit to the authority of some central team that they are not involved in. The church is led by a team of elders; this team has authority over the whole church and it includes people from each of the sites. When a new elder is recognised, they are not simply appointed an elder of their site but of the whole church. The primary function of the elders is providing security in the church and guarding the doctrine, teaching, mission and unity of the church. Because the elders are represented in every site, they can maintain high levels of local ownership for the central vision while ensuring that local challenges and concerns are represented centrally.

Practically speaking, many people are surprised to learn that our eldership team only meets three or four times a year, and that when we do meet, a large portion of our time together is spent eating curry and praying! The discussions that we have tend to be on quite high-level theology or philosophy of ministry topics.

Alongside these meetings though, we have worked very hard to develop good friendships with one another, and we chat a lot informally, ensuring we are all on the same page in exercising our shared authority together well. Every now and then we need to call an impromptu meeting if something big is happening in the church, but we have found the need for such meetings to be infrequent.

Whilst the authority in the church resides with the elders, the practical outworking of leadership that most members of the church experience is through their site leaders. These site leaders will be heavily involved in the communities that their sites are trying to reach and will have day-to-day responsibility for leading the site in living out the church's mission. Site leaders are appointed by the elders, and are usually either elders themselves or are in the process of becoming elders. They lead with a team of others in the site, and these teams are often defined quite loosely with plenty of flexibility to adapt to the particular needs of the site.

This way of doing things works well for us because we are deliberate in empowering the site leaders, and the elders exercise their authority with a light touch. Site leaders choose what is preached about at their site, and who does that preaching; they raise up their own volunteers and teams; they programme their own community and mission activities; and they are able to step into the vast majority of functions of church leadership, whilst still having the safety net of the elders to fall back on. Because of this we are able to raise up and unleash young and unproven leaders, and support them as they grow into the stature of leadership on the job.

We have found that this model of church-wide eldership wielding a light touch, plus site leadership teams that carry much of the day-to-day leadership responsibility, frees up capacity in the 'centre' to focus on the advance and multiplication of new sites. I myself do not personally lead any of our sites. Instead I use my time coaching our leaders, pioneering new sites and making myself available as a resource to support other churches. For many churches, multiplication is an afterthought, and I am so grateful that we have been able to structure in a way that allows missional advance to form a central component of our strategy. I am not saying that this cannot happen if the senior leader is also leading a site, but careful thought must be given to where the pioneering impulse will come from and how it can stay at the heart of what the church is doing.

The final element in our leadership team is our trustees. This is a team that operates centrally and I am indebted to them for their outstanding work in establishing best practice in legal, safeguarding, employment and governance areas.

Culture: Central Identity, Local Contextualisation

It is impossible to underestimate how important culture is in a church (or any other organisation). Culture is simply another way of saying 'how things are around here'. It is about the look and feel of what things are actually like in your church. It is not what you aspire to be but simply what you are. Culture is something that you can work to shape, but it is not easy, nor is it quick. I have come to see that of all the things that we can do on a human level, culture is the one on which everything stands or falls. For this reason, shaping a culture that is shared by all of our sites is a high priority for me.

We have identified seven key cultural distinctives which characterise the CCM 'vibe'. I believe that these have been instrumental in how we have built so far. These cultural distinctives are:

- A Second Chance Culture
- A Have a Go Culture
- A Think the Best Culture
- A Forward Looking Culture
- A Generous Culture
- A Wholehearted Culture
- A Good Food Culture

Because these cultural distinctives are so important to our multiplanting approach, I will unpack them in much greater detail in section two of this book. For now, it is important to understand that culture flows from the centre, and is then contextualised into our different sites.

How this works can be illustrated by an example. One of our cultural distinctives is a Good Food Culture, and this is shared by all of our sites. What this means is that every site places a premium on food, hospitality and inclusion. We want to make sure that people feel welcome. This is often expressed by putting on nice food at our services and events. How we actually do this in practice differs from one site to the next, based on the people in the site with their passions and gifts, and also based on the nature of the community that they are trying to reach. For one of our sites this is expressed by frequently providing bacon butties before the services. Another site has raised the bar in serving 'world class cake' at Sunday meetings. Still another site frequently has 'bring and share' community lunches. The culture is the same, but the way the sites express it is individually contextualised. The same is true for each of the cultural points.

Sundays: Central Blueprint, Local Flavour

I was once sitting in a training session with Nicky Gumbel, where people were asking him questions about ideas they had for adapting the Alpha Course. Nicky explained that it had been created in a way that works, and advised people to try running it his way before making any changes, so they could see for themselves why it works so well and would then be in a position to understand the impact that doing things differently would have.

I think this is great advice that extends well beyond Alpha, and I feel a similar way about our Sunday meetings. Over the years we have developed a way of doing Sundays that works really well for us. It is a fun and inspiring time where people meet with God, make new friends and are challenged from the Word. I think of this as a blueprint for a CCM Sunday, and I will run through the elements of it in greater depth in chapter 16. When we start a new site, I expect that site to run their Sunday meetings in this way, at least initially. It creates a consistency of environment across the church and helps them to understand the CCM way of doing things. Of course there is a place for experimentation and new ideas, but the blueprint that we have created gives us a great starting point for what we do in our gathered meetings.

Despite all of our services working to the same blueprint, each of our sites also carries a unique flavour. This is inevitable as the preaching, leading and music are all done by people in that site, and they do so using their own styles. Some of our preachers are funnier than others, some are more energetic, some are born storytellers, some are thorough expositors and others have a very pastoral approach. We want to make sure we are all learning from each other's strengths, but we also want all of our preachers to be employing their own personal styles, and doing so effectively. This naturally means that each of our sites has a distinct flavour.

Similarly, our musicians have different influences and styles. We are reaching into communities with different musical tastes, and many of our worship leaders are writing their own songs and giving their own expression to the journey that God is taking us on. Again, all of this creates a very different flavour in each of our meetings, and we are very happy to embrace and celebrate this.

Money: Central Resources, Local Flexibility

Not all of the communities in which Christ Church Manchester has sites are demographically similar. Our first site was in one of the most deprived areas in England, and the second was in the middle of studentland. The next two were in areas that are more suburban, where people are, on average, a little bit wealthier. Our fifth site is right in the centre of the city, where rich and poor people exist side by side. This means that the income generated through regular giving at each of the sites is not equal. We don't believe that better-off communities should end up with heavily resourced churches just because they can pay for it, while poor people end up with the scraps, and it has long been a dream of ours to see resources (and people) flowing into the neediest areas of our city.

As a church, we have one bank account and one budget. This budget does assign certain funds for each site to spend, and sets targets for giving in each site, but the budgeted income at a site is not used as the basis for what that site can spend. Rather, we look at the needs and opportunities in that site and budget accordingly. Some of the sites will end up being net contributors to the budget and others net recipients. This is part of the beauty of operating as one church across many sites.

We have also found ourselves able to give big chunks of money away, and in November each year we receive a special offering for poor people, which last year generated the equivalent of more than two months' worth of regular church income, all of which was given away to those in need. We have found that many people who have very little show incredible generosity when given the opportunity to help meet the needs of others.

Whilst the budget for each site is determined centrally, site leaders have lots of scope to determine what that money is spent on. A suggested breakdown is provided of how the funding has been assigned, but site leaders have flexibility to spend more than the allotted amounts in one area, so long as they are willing to spend less in another area.

These are just a few examples of how we decide what to hold centrally and what to hold locally. There is a constant need as new opportunities arise to make these kinds of decisions, and it is definitely a skill learned with time. The principles suggested here form a good guide for how we approach other issues too; if something is 'mission-critical' where it matters that it is done in a certain way, then we will make a decision centrally that will be rolled out into all of our sites. On the other hand, when something requires speed of movement and flexibility of approach, then we want it to be handled at a local level in a way that works for the context. I have been able to build a team of leaders that appreciates the value of both the central and the local. Developing these two-way relationships of trust has proved to be pivotal in making multiplanting work.

Chapter Four:
How We Keep on Starting
New Sites

Over the thirty years that I have been starting new churches, one of the things that I have seen every single time is that church planting comes with a cost. This is most obviously felt by the pioneers who are on the ground. They have stepped away from circumstances that are familiar and comfortable, often from fruitful ministry where they were able to play to their strengths, and embarked on a journey into the unknown where they find themselves starting again relationally, battling feelings of isolation and needing to grind something out of nothing.

Less obvious, but no less important, is the cost that is borne by the sending congregation. They have invested significant resources, both money and people, in establishing the new plant. Those left behind often find that some of their close friends are no longer around, that some of the gifted and passionate people who were building with them have left a vacuum, and that the focus of vision and prayer has been on something happening 'out there'. This can leave a feeling of inertia in the original congregation. We have come to refer to this price paid by those left behind when a church plant goes as 'the rip effect'.

The fact that church planting is costly is no reason not to do it. I have seen that many congregations will joyfully pay this price for the sake of Christ's mission. I have also noticed that once a congregation has planted and experienced this rip effect, the high cost can often deter them from planting again any time soon. The emotional burden of constantly building friendships with people, only for them to be sent out somewhere else, the ministry cost of raising up new leaders, preachers and musicians whose ministry you will never reap the benefits of, and the vision cost of always talking about the 'next thing' that will not directly involve the majority of your people starts to stack up. People can begin to feel that stability is required for a time, rather than further pioneering.

This is also true in churches that build with a multisite model, particularly if one of those sites is considered to be the 'central' or 'main' site. That site absorbs the cost of each of the new sites, and the church tends to reach about three or four sites before progress is stalled because the sending capacity of that central site has been exhausted. My dream has always been to start twenty churches in Manchester, and to even get close to this I have had to find a way to deal with the rip effect without doing too much damage to the churches that we already have.

The way we get a new site started is through a four-step process that has been described as 'lean and scalable'. Because we start lean, we minimise the rip effect that each new site has on the others. That is not to say there is no pain at all, but there is much less than there might otherwise be. We call the model multi*planting* because our new sites really do have more in common with church plants than with traditional new sites in a multisite model, and rather than hiving off a big chunk of an existing congregation to start the new meeting, we identify a small handful of pioneers and commission them to gather people into a new community. A few of the people they gather may come from existing sites, but this is spread across all the sites, meaning there is not too much of a burden on any one, and many of them are people who are not currently part of any of our sites (often they have been out of church for a while or have just moved to the area). The low start-up costs of just a few pioneers and a bare-bones financial investment (as discussed in the previous chapter), along with the limited impact that each new site has on the existing ones, means that the ceiling for repeated planting disappears, and we have developed a planting model that is truly scalable and that we could continue to use in the coming years to plant dozens of new sites across the city.

Four Stages of a Plant

We have tended to approach planting a new site as a four-step process that can be represented by a baseball diamond.

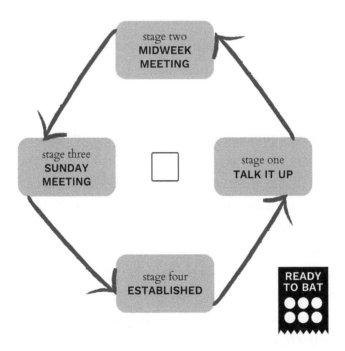

STAGE ONE: Talk It Up

Our first stage is making a lot of noise about our intention to plant in a new area. We often do this straight away after launching a Sunday meeting in one place, when our people are frequently asking the question, 'where next?' In practice, it looks a bit like what I described earlier about how we launched Bolton Family Church as an act of faith during a prayer meeting. We will publicly declare our intent to plant into an area, casually dropping it into our existing Sunday meetings, our prayer gatherings, our digital communication and our one-on-one conversations.

What we are trying to do through this is to unearth a few people who feel stirred by God that this is for them. By making this kind of noise, we create an atmosphere of faith for a new endeavour and we will try to put on some kind of informal event for people to explore their interest further, which could be anything from a curry and chat, to a prayer meeting at a home in the area. We are looking to get to the point where we have four or five people who are interested in trying to make something happen in that particular community.

One of the questions that I am most frequently asked about this stage of our process is how we decide which is the next plant that we will talk up. The truth is that we always have quite a few ideas about places that we would like to plant (see 'ready to bat' on the diagram) and we need to select one of those options to create a bit of buzz about. There can be different factors that influence the choices we make about where to plant, but we are essentially just trying to get an answer that sits well in our spirit and feels like the natural next place to go. These different factors are well illustrated by the last few sites that we planted.

At the time of writing, the most recent place that we have launched a site is in Manchester city centre. For us this was quite a strategic choice. It's a part of the city with lots happening and provides an opportunity to reach into lots of different communities, including creative culture-makers, entrepreneurs and young professionals, students, and people who struggle with poverty and/or addictions. We are also aware that, to this point, we have planted sites in South and East Manchester, and we see the city centre site as something that can open doors to further plants that reach into new communities in the northern and western of the city.

The site we launched before the city centre one was CCM Kingsway. This was less of a strategic choice for us, and more of a response to a prophetic word that we were given in a prayer meeting. We were gathered with leaders of other churches from across the UK and somebody shared a word with us, naming a specific part of Manchester as a place that would be important for us. As we prayed into this word, we believed that God was speaking to us, so we started gathering in the area that he had said. This eventually became our Kingsway site.

The next site that we will be talking up is CCM Wythenshawe. This is not because of any prophecy or strategic plan, but rather the response to an opportunity that has presented itself. We have a vision-filled leader already living there and a few other people in the area, so it seems obvious to try to get a site started in this community. Not every site that we talk up in this way ends up working out, and we are OK with that. Making a bit of noise and seeing what response we get is part of our process of weighing up our next move, and if it doesn't quite take off then we just go back to the drawing board and talk up somewhere else instead! We have found that they work out as we hoped more often than they don't.

We have learned that it is only viable to have one plant at this first stage. If we are trying to share vision for too many things at the same time then we only end up confusing people and none of it really sticks. There may still be others starting to build and gather in other parts of the city, but this happens under the radar so that it doesn't distract from the one we are talking up. Even as we cast vision for Wythenshawe, we have a couple of other leaders dreaming and praying about planting into the areas they are living in, but we are clear that we can only really push the vision for one new plant at once, and it is not until that one gets up and running that we can start to give more profile to the next one. Having several plants ready to go at once is a great problem to have, but it is something that we have had to build into the culture of the church over many years.

STAGE TWO: Midweek Meeting

I know the 'talking it up' phase of a new site has been successful when I have found a few people who feel interested in doing something. My next step is to start a regular midweek meeting in the place that we are trying to reach that will serve as a gathering point as we build.

This was exactly the approach that I took with Susan in Bolton after I had 'planted' Bolton Family Church in that prayer meeting. Susan agreed to open up her home and she had a few friends living near her who she was able to invite. I drove over from Manchester each week with a car-load of people and we met, ate and prayed. Over time friendships were formed, more locals were gathered and a church community was built.

We may still meet in a home at this stage if necessary, but as time has gone by I have come to prefer a more public meeting in a venue like a coffee shop or pub function room. This raises the profile a bit from our regular 'community groups', puts a stake of intent in the ground and removes a barrier of entry for newcomers who want to visit. Turning up to a coffee shop doesn't feel quite as intimidating as going to a stranger's house!

When I am trying to gather people to this meeting, I am not very picky at all about who turns up. It is a mistake to only look for those who feel a long-term call to the new plant. If I find somebody who is willing to give us one evening a week for six months to help us get something started, then I will gratefully accept their offer, even if they won't be with us for the long-haul. It might be that by having them around for a bit it allows us to run a viable meeting that leads us to find those that do feel called to it long-term.

One of the big things that I am looking for in this stage of the plant is somebody who can lead the site when we launch Sunday meetings. When I am first setting up the midweek group I find somebody who is organised enough to pull together a meeting each week and hospitable enough to create a fun atmosphere, and ask them to make the midweek group happen. They are a bridgehead for us into the new community, but this doesn't necessarily mean they will be asked to lead the site as it moves into the next stages. I make it very clear to them that what I am asking is simply to run a meeting for a year, and this gives us all some space to discern where God is leading us as we go. Once a leader is in place, and they have gathered fifteen to twenty people (sometimes slightly fewer), we begin looking at the next stage: starting a Sunday meeting.

STAGE THREE: Sunday Meeting

When we reach the point where we are ready to launch a Sunday meeting, we are pretty sure that the plant is going to work. Our leader and team are in place, and the next thing that's needed is a venue. In choosing one, there are a few important qualities that we are looking for: somewhere relatively cheap, of a good size (obviously not too small, but also not too big – there is nothing worse than twenty people rattling around in a room that holds 200), in a location that is easy to find, with appropriate kids' work space and storage. Beyond this we are not too fussy and we have found that venues like schools, socials clubs, hotels and old chapels have all worked well for us.

Trying to run meetings with a fairly small team is a challenge, and if a few key people are away then it can make the room feel rather empty. This is where we lean into the strength of being part of a wider whole and we draft in some reinforcements from our other sites. We 'borrow' a few people (ideally from sites that meet at a different time of day) and ask them to double up for a few months, bulking out our meetings and helping the new site reach the critical mass for a viable meeting quickly. There is an element of 'fake it till you make it' about this approach, but it has proved very helpful to us and has given a bit of breathing space for our new sites to grow in their own right. In a similar vein, we will also borrow preachers and musicians from other sites, and we can draw on the skill and gifting of a wide range of people to supplement those who are part of the planting group.

The Sunday meetings in our new site follow a very similar pattern to all of our other sites (see chapter 16). We know that in the early days people are unlikely to be attracted to a new plant because of spectacular Sunday worship services, but we do want everyone who walks through the door to experience teaching that they can connect with and worship that helps them engage with God. Alongside this we put a very high premium on hospitality and community. When there is just a small number, people have the opportunity to help newcomers feel like part of the community very quickly, and this is one of the biggest assets of a church at this stage.

STAGE FOUR: Established

Unlike the earlier stages, there isn't a clear point when a site moves from stage three to stage four. It is something that happens gradually over time, involving a number of factors: there is a bit of numerical growth involved (we tend to shoot for communities of fifty to eighty people, so an established site would be something approaching this); the need to 'borrow' people, preachers and musicians from other sites disappears; there is a growth to multiple community groups; and more leaders are raised up within the site. A good test to apply is to look how much the meeting suffers if the primary leader is not there.

We don't put strict financial obligations on each site (see chapter 17) as the circumstances of each community are different, but we are looking to see established sites reach financial maturity, with people giving generously. Ideally, most of our established sites will be net contributors to our church finances, creating a surplus to give away to the needy, serve the wider church, invest in foreign mission and pioneer other new sites.

We want all of our sites, whatever stage they are at, to own the vision of planting across the city, but it is our established sites that are in a position to shoulder the load. Much of the pioneering impulse, as well as the resourcing of newer sites with people and prayer, comes from sites that are already established. Each new site opens up new possibilities for further planting as people gather to it from neighbouring communities.

Seeing these four stages helps us pace our planting well. At our current pace we are starting a new site every two years. We have found that spending a few months talking a site up, and then just over a year meeting midweek, usually brings us to the point where we are ready to start a Sunday meeting. It tends to be between a year and a half and two years after we launch on Sundays that the site starts to feel like it is becoming established. At the moment this pace is working well for us, but it will be interesting to see if this pace quickens as we continue to grow and our planting capacity increases.

Putting It into Practice

Over my forty years in ministry, I can't count the number of books that I have read about ministry, church and leadership. Some of those books have shaken my world and given me a completely new way of looking at things. Others served to reinforce what I was already doing and reassure me that I was on the right track. And there were those that seemed to advocate a way of doing things that wouldn't be easy to implement in my own context, even though I liked the heart behind it.

In recent years, the number of new ideas, models and philosophies that we are all exposed to has increased at a seemingly exponential rate. It is easier than ever to visit rapidly growing churches, to fill our diaries with leadership conferences, to skype with leaders from around the world, and to stay up to date on podcasts, blogs and tweets. There are so many new ways of doing things that it can leave us feeling a bit overloaded with information and uncertain where to start. I guess by writing this book, I have just added to that!

When I give my time to reading a book or visiting a conference, I consider it time well spent if I come away with one new thought that moves me in the direction that I am trying to go. Even when I am totally gripped with where an author wants to lead me, I know that leading my church into something new isn't a quick or an easy process. At the end of each suggestion, I want to give you some thoughts on where to start with multiplanting and provoke your thinking. Whether you are leading something that is working, are feeling stuck or are yet to step out, my hope and prayer is that you will find something, even a single thought, that can help you step forward into God's purposes for you.

Start with Vision

Reflecting back on my own multiplanting journey, things didn't start for me with a ministry model or even with a plan. It started that day in my car listening to Steve Nicholson preach and screaming at my stereo, 'I want to plant twenty churches!' To put things another way, it all started when God touched my heart with a vision that was about more than building up a single church, but being involved in a movement that could reach a whole region. At the time, I couldn't articulate exactly what it would look like or what would need to be done. But like Abraham when he had been called by God, I knew that I needed to get moving, and I had faith that God would show me what I needed to know along the way. The combination of vision for what can be and faith that God will lead as you go is a powerful combination to get a movement started!

A lot of the work that I do involves travelling around the country consulting with church leadership teams and helping them through challenging times. One of the most common issues that comes up in these times is when forward momentum in the church has stalled and nobody quite knows what to do to get things moving again. Whenever I see this challenge emerge, the first questions I ask are about vision. I want to know what are the things that keep people awake at night and get them up in the morning. I often find that in churches that are stuck, issues of maintenance are brought to centre stage and can crowd out the pioneering zeal for seeing the kingdom of God spread through a region. Suggestions of planting a new church or starting a new ministry are rebuffed with concerns for how they would impact existing rotas, and the pioneering impulse is stifled.

Without vision it is impossible to advance. This vision can come from many places, but it is cultivated above all through prayer and intimacy with the Father. It was through his extended early morning prayer that Jesus became clear that he should move on from Capernaum to the other towns – 'for that is what [he] came for' (Mark 1:38). It was also through prayer and fasting that the church in Antioch were led to send out Paul and Barnabas to take the gospel to new towns and cities in previously unreached regions (Acts 13:3).

This vision for the next place drove the apostolic mission. In each region, Paul chose the most prominent town and preached the good news about Jesus, and as people believed, a church community was formed there and Paul moved on to the next place. As I noted earlier, Paul didn't personally bring the gospel to every village and hamlet in the region, and yet he still considered that the gospel had been 'fulfilled' there. The expectation was that by starting a church in the city, he had established a gospel base from which a whole region could be reached.

This was the fundamental shift that occurred in my thinking as I drove north. No longer was a single church in a village enough for me. I dreamed of reaching all of the towns and cities of Greater Manchester. My ministry had become bigger than my church, because my vision had become bigger.

Multiplanting is one approach to answering the question of how we can reach a large city or region with the gospel. It is not the only approach, nor even necessarily the best approach in every context, but the questions it addresses are ones to which we must have an answer:

How big is your vision? Do you have dreams beyond your own church of reaching the region in which you are based? What are you doing to turn those dreams into reality?

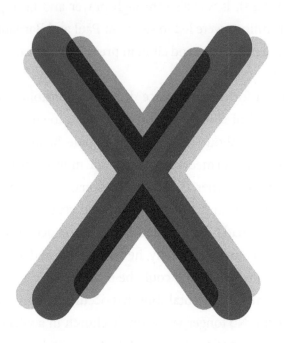

Part Two:
Multiplanting Culture

In the first section of this book, I have tried to describe what I mean by multiplanting and share a bit of my journey. As I have outlined the things that we have done and our approach to centralisation and to starting new sites, it has had quite a strategic feel to it. I don't apologise for this. Our strategy has been a very important factor (humanly speaking) in how we have got this far. But strategy is only the second most important factor. In first place is culture. As it has been said, 'Culture eats strategy for breakfast.'[5]

When I talk about culture, what I mean is simply 'the way we do things around here'. It is the set of shared attitudes and behaviours that shape what we do. This is not the same as values, which tend to be conceptual priorities rather than specific ways of doing things. It is also not the same as vision, which is more of an aspiration of what you would like to see happen than a description of how things are. Culture is about the way things are done right now, and every church has a culture, whether it has been deliberately crafted or not.

The good news is that culture can be shaped, but this is not a simple or quick process. Doing a preaching series on your desired culture may be a reasonable start, but it is far from sufficient. Building culture is a process that takes years of constant reinforcement, but that can be lost in mere months if it is neglected.

Sometimes I think that all I do is build culture and help other leaders to do the same. This may sound a bit dramatic, but even when I don't realise it I am building culture. Whether at home, at church, or even walking my dog with friends, I am contributing to culture building. It is a long process that must be reinforced every day for years before it takes hold. I think it is quite telling in the biblical account that when Daniel and the other Jewish elites were taken from Israel to Babylon, their first three years were spent being educated and immersed in Babylonian culture; this tallies with my own experience of how long cultural formation takes.

Over time, as group members begin to experience the good of a culture in their relationships, it can become a subconscious way of relating to each other. Though teaching has a place, culture is caught more than it is taught. This means that it is imperative for the leader to live out the culture that they speak of. You are the visual aid that will reinforce the culture that you are building. In the end, what you build will be a reflection of the culture of your church, and if you want to pioneer and reach a whole region, this must be at the heart of your culture. At Christ Church Manchester, we talk about the seven distinctives of our culture, and these distinctives are the key to our whole approach to ministry. In my opinion, it is the culture that we have developed that has enabled us to build a church that can continue to pioneer new sites into more and more communities, all the while enjoying the strength and unity that comes from being one church for the city.

These are our cultural distinctives:

A Second Chance Culture. Failure isn't fatal, and whether people have messed up morally or taken a ministry risk that hasn't worked out, we want to help them get back on their feet and go again.

A Have a Go Culture. We are always up for trying new things, and we know that sometimes they will work out and sometimes they won't. We are quick to give people opportunities to use their skills and take some responsibility.

A Think the Best Culture. In our relationships we look for each other's positive qualities, assume good intentions and seek to draw out the best in one another.

A Generous Culture. As a church we want to give our best away. We want to be open-handed with our energy, our people, our time and our resources and use it all to bless others and build God's kingdom.

A Forward Looking Culture. We have big dreams for the future and embrace change. We are entrepreneurial and are full of faith. We love creating culture and embracing new technology and ideas as we build.

A Wholehearted Culture. We are very enthusiastic about serving God. We throw ourselves fully into our worship, our discipleship, our community and the mission Jesus has given to us.

A Good Food Culture. Food is a big deal for us. Lots of what we do is around a table and we prize hospitality highly.

In the next few chapters I will unpack in much more detail how these cultural distinctives have been key to building a multiplanting church.

Chapter Five:
A Second Chance
Culture

When I moved up to Manchester with a dream of planting twenty new churches, I was not new to church planting. As I have said, I had already had a couple of attempts at starting new churches, with less than stellar results. Neither really got much traction, with one of them eventually closing years later, and I had made quite a few mistakes along the way. I didn't inspire much confidence as a church planter, and I am forever thankful to God for his patience and kindness with me, that those stuttering first attempts were not the end of the journey for me.

Sadly, there are lots of people who haven't been given as many chances as I have. Sometimes in church we can struggle to know what to do with those who have tried and failed, who have made mistakes, who have fallen into sinful behaviour, or who have simply given up. While the example of Jesus is clear, in practice these people can end up left on the sidelines without any real part to play or restoration track to progress on.

There is an often-told story about C.S. Lewis walking in on a discussion where experts from around the world were trying to work out what was unique about Christianity. 'Oh, that's easy,' Lewis apparently said, 'It's grace.' Christianity is about grace. We are brought into God's family, not because we deserve it (we don't) but because he gives it as a gift. Even when we were far away, he sought us and found us, and in the ultimate act of grace, Jesus laid down his very life in our place, for our sins.

Jesus taught about grace a lot. Often the way he did so was wrapped up in stories and parables, and these stories carry an interesting challenge for those who have received grace. In a story in Matthew 18, there is a person who owes a large sum of money to a king, and he has no chance of being able to repay his debt. He falls on his knees and begs, and the king forgives him the debt. The same man who has just received such mercy then encounters someone else who owes him a small amount of money and is not able to repay it. In the story, the man is harsh and ruthless and insists on repayment, unwilling to apply the same mercy that he himself has received. Grace is supposed to be contagious, and when we receive the astonishing grace of God, this makes all the difference to the way we treat one another.

At Christ Church Manchester, a phrase that we have developed to describe the grace of God in practice in our community is Second Chance Culture. To put it simply, this means that there is space to make mistakes, learn and grow without being shut out in the cold the moment things start to go wrong. If we are going to continue planting across our city, we will need dozens of pioneers, preachers, leaders, musicians and Spirit-filled men and women ready and eager to play their part. We simply can't afford to leave people on the sidelines whenever something goes wrong. We need to make sure we have pathways of healing and restoration for people to brush themselves off and go again. We realise that as we give responsibility to a wide range of people, from brand new Christians to seasoned believers, there will be moments when the going gets tough and people will let us down. When this happens, we do our best not to shy away from giving them more opportunities, because we believe that people grow and mature as they serve, both through their triumphs and through their failures.

A Second Chance Culture and Sin

The Second Chance Culture works on multiple levels. First, there is the level of moral failure and sinful behaviour. Obviously, sin is a very bad thing and we don't want to condone or encourage it, but nor do we want to write people off and leave them on the scrapheap because of bad decisions and mistakes they have made. The Bible is full of people who have done some very shady things and yet still have a big part to play in God's story. I am in awe of a God who prospered Abraham, even when through fear he told a half-truth about his wife that resulted in her being condemned to be part of Pharaoh's harem! Abraham lied, deceived and clearly lacked trust in God, and yet God still blessed him and had a big part for him in the unfolding story.

Time and again we see the redemption stories of broken and flawed people being gently healed and restored by God's grace. Our Second Chance Culture makes a big difference to the way we deal with moral issues that arise; there is no place for punishment, but rather for hope-filled repentance, rebuilding and restoration, and then going again stronger and wiser than before.

Every year we run an Introduction to Preaching course where we share some basics with potential future preachers. The course concludes with people being given the opportunity to deliver a short sample talk to the group that is recorded for their site leader to listen to at a later date. A couple of minutes into her talk, one young woman on the course realised that she had forgotten something that she meant to say, and so she stopped the talk, panicked and exclaimed, 'Oh, ****!' Obviously, this language has no place in a sermon, nor on the lips of a believer more generally, but we could see from the look on her face that she was devastated at what had come out from her mouth, and we could also see that the moment presented an opportunity to show the Second Chance Culture in action. As a group we laughed it off and showed her how to delete the recording, and the group leader made a joke about nobody mentioning it to her site leader. She started again and did a very good job with the talk, and has since had the opportunity to speak in our Sunday meetings.

This may seem like a small example, and in other circumstances the journey of repentance and restoration may take considerably longer, but it is a journey that we want to go on with people. I find it striking when I read the narrative of the disciples beginning to realise that Jesus has risen from the dead, how often Peter is singled out. Peter, of course, failed Jesus in a big way the night before Jesus died, and yet John points out that after hearing the report from Mary Magdalene, 'Peter went out with the other disciple, and they were going towards the tomb. Both of them were running' (John 20:3-4). I love this image of Peter sprinting towards the tomb to embrace the Lord he failed. Whatever may have happened in their past, if somebody is running to Jesus then they are someone that I can work with!

Jesus embraced Peter back into the fold, and restored him with breakfast on the beach and a fresh commissioning. Within weeks, Peter was preaching the gospel on the day of Pentecost, and leading the church. There was no need for restoration to be drawn out in this case. It took as long as it took, and when it was done, Peter was back in the game and ready to go again.

A Second Chance Culture and Relationships

The Second Chance Culture also works on the level of relationships. Unfortunately, there will always be times when people will let one another down, but as a church we want to be quick to extend a hand of forgiveness and friendship. Perhaps the most famous of all Jesus' stories is the parable of the prodigal son. In this story, a son demands his share of the family inheritance while his father is still alive (essentially wishing his dad dead), and then he blows it all on wild parties. In terms of dishonour and insult, this is about as extreme as it can get, particularly in the culture of the day. Yet rather than holding it against the son, the father eagerly longs for his return, looks out for him and runs to him with a great big hug, before throwing a party the day he does find him. Even though the boy had broken the relationship, the father was willing to welcome him home with another chance.

A few years ago one of my team came to me with something that had arisen in a meeting with the leadership team of his site. He had only just been brought into that team, and on one issue that arose the discussion got rather heated. I think he was expecting me to bring some practical wisdom into the specific question, or to play referee in the dispute, but to his surprise my only advice was that he should apologise for his part in the meeting (without expecting any apologies in return). He took my advice, and his apology was well received. The issue was quickly resolved, and by being willing to show humility and reach out with an apology, this young guy won favour and influence with the team, and the site was strengthened by a new-found unity that had been forged amongst its leaders. This is what we want to embody in our Second Chance Culture – being quick to apologise and quick to forgive.

A Second Chance Culture and Ministry

One of the most common reasons that I have noticed for people feeling cut off in church life is when they have had a go at a particular ministry role, and then are not asked to do it again, sometimes without an explanation. One of my friends once told the story of when he first preached in his church. 'Colin,' he said, 'I was awful. I made no sense. I used Scripture badly. I wandered around aimlessly at the front and everybody felt sorry for me. Not a good morning!' As we talked, I realised that he had been given very little training in how to write or deliver a talk, and then after his poor first attempt he was told that he couldn't preach again for another eighteen months. He was devastated! He desired to preach, and he wanted help. What could he possibly learn from this experience?

Sadly, my friend's experience is not an uncommon one, and it illustrates why a Second Chance Culture is so important as people step out in ministry. As leaders, we need to take a level of personal responsibility for the unsuccessful attempts of those whom we are working with. When somebody tries something new and it doesn't go well for whatever reason, the question that I always ask is, 'What did I do (or not do) that contributed to this?' It is far too easy to write somebody off for a bad talk or a failed small group when the problem was most likely in the mentoring, delegation and management of that individual or situation. Rather than cast the individual aside, I would rather take responsibility myself, do things differently next time and give the individual another go with better support. If there is no improvement (or particularly if there is no teachability) there may eventually come a time to look at transitioning the individual out of the role, but I have found that in many contexts this can be done way too hastily.

Another thing that I have noticed is senior leaders typecasting those who have tried and failed in the past, blinding them to the possibility of the person changing or maturing. Even Paul appeared to do this after John Mark had let him down on one of his church planting journeys (Acts 15:37-40). Paul's reluctance to take him on the next trip may be understandable, but what John Mark needed was the restoration and second chance that Barnabas offered him. Barnabas refused to write off John Mark and he gave him the opportunity to prove that he had matured and had a useful role to play in the mission. In time, even Paul saw the change in John Mark and valued him as an important co-worker.

I feel very passionate about this, because when people are cast aside after one or two unsuccessful attempts, everybody loses: the individual retreats into their shell, licking their wounds and reluctant to volunteer for anything again in future, and the church suffers from a perpetual shortage of workers, despite having a long list of people on the sidelines who they deem 'unsuitable' for whatever reason.

A Second Chance Culture and Maturity

Maturity is a fascinating concept to me, and I can't help thinking that it is often misunderstood or misappropriated in our churches today. I have often thought about the topic in relation to Jesus' disciples. It seems like they were more 'mature' on the day they first heard Jesus' call and dropped their nets to follow than they were after three years with him when they returned to their nets out of fear, despondency and disappointment. I don't for a second believe that being with Jesus didn't cause the disciples to grow in maturity, but the observation does challenge some of our perceptions of what mature discipleship looks like. In his resurrected state, Jesus spent significant time restoring his disciples and preparing them for all that was to come in the book of Acts.

Paul addresses the topic of maturity in his letter to the Ephesian church, and he does so in the context of God-gifted ministries being used to prepare the people of God for works of service. During times of preparation, people can often seem very mature, but it is only as they step out on God's mission that this maturity is put to the test. Like many things in life, maturity is worked out in serving communities, and in time is exposed for what it is, developed, stretched and refined, until it attains to the whole measure of the fullness of Christ. Now, that's maturity!

Often senior leaders have a well-meaning desire to protect our people from the painful hardships of ministry. We can do this out of love as we remember our own steep learning curves, but by doing so we can leave them with a superficial 'maturity' and deny them those same formative experiences that grew us, deepened us and brought us to true maturity through the pain. Maturity is forged on the front lines of the battle, and so we must resist the temptation to make maturity a prerequisite for ministry.

One of the ways that we talk about this at Christ Church Manchester is by saying that we have both a 'very high bar' and a 'very low bar'. The high bar is aspirational and describes the standard that we hold out for discipleship. We are wholehearted in pursuit of God and don't want to settle for compromise in our walks with him. As we look to work with believers, we recognise there are always new steps that we can take in our faith journeys,

74

and we urge and support everyone to a very high standard of love, faith and devotion. At the same time, we have a very low bar of getting started. We want to create opportunities for people to do meaningful things, even when their lives are still messy (we take our cue here from the opportunities that Jesus gave to the twelve). We believe that it is through these opportunities that people will begin to learn, grow and move towards the high bar.

I think that this way of thinking of two bars proves way more effective at helping people grow towards maturity than the more common approach of a single bar that is somewhere in the middle; high enough to exclude people from ministry who may otherwise have a role to play, and low enough to allow those who have reached it to settle into a superficial (and frankly dull) middle of the road Christianity rather than being continuously stretched on the journey of faith.

A Second Chance Culture and Failure

There have been more than a few moments on our journey where we have tried something that just hasn't worked (we will talk more about this in the next chapter), but our Second Chance Culture creates a safe space for us to try things that might not come off and to do so without recriminations. When something doesn't work, there can be many reasons for it and we want to understand those reasons and learn from them to give us the best shot next time.

We make a big effort to ensure that people who are involved in pioneering new initiatives understand that if it doesn't work, that is fine by us and it certainly won't be held against them (if anything, we respect them more for their willingness to give it a shot). Over the years there have been a number of new sites that we have tried to start that have reached stage one (talking it up) or stage two (midweek meeting), but never quite got going. Whenever this has happened, the person leading them has had another go and applied the lessons they have learned to make a success of the next site they plant. It is inevitable that as we pioneer there will be times for all of us where we give something our best try and for whatever reason it doesn't quite work out. But with a Second Chance Culture, these moments are turned from disasters into springboards, and we make sure there are plenty more opportunities for those involved to take responsibility and try again in the future.

Chapter Six:
A Have a Go Culture

When I returned to the UK from my time in America, I took leadership of a small church on the east side of Manchester and spent the next couple of years helping this church grow and become established. My dream was always continued multiplication, and thus, within a year or so, I was beginning to look at and pray about how we could plant our next congregation. I was feeling stirred by God that we should try to do something in Fallowfield, the heart of Manchester's studentland.

My prayers were answered in early 2009 when I was introduced to Tim and Vicki Simmonds, a couple who had been living in the Midlands and who had been developing a dream of their own of planting a church among the students of Manchester. Later that year, Tim and Vicki made the move north with their family to join with us. Tim outlined a plan to settle into the city, learn how the church worked, and then maybe in a year's time start planting. I listened politely, smiled and nodded, and then said to him, 'Find a room, find a worship leader, and let's have a go'. Two months later, our first site plant was up and running.

This approach might seem a bit strange to some people, but it flows out of something that is at the core of who we are: the Have a Go Culture. This probably needs a little bit of explaining. Because we know that God has made promises for the future, we are willing to step out and try things in the present that might work and might not, knowing that ultimately, by his power, the promises will be fulfilled. We do our best not to take silly risks on the way, but we would rather step out and have a go, even if it doesn't work, than sit back and do nothing. At least that way we have learned a few lessons and are better equipped to succeed next time.

A Have a Go Culture and Adventure

One of my favourite biblical examples of the adventurous nature of faith is the story of Jonathan and his armour bearer that is found in 1 Samuel 13 and 14. At this point in history, God's people were stuck. They were at war with the Philistines and were losing, so the people were hiding in holes, caves and cisterns. The king had been rejected by God for disobeying a direct command. The Israelites were outnumbered and unarmed. Only two of them (King Saul and his son Jonathan) were allowed to possess swords, and everybody else had to go cap in hand to the Philistines even to get their farm equipment sharpened.

Whilst few (if any) of us will have experienced a situation as extreme as the one faced by the Israelites, we can often find ourselves getting stuck in church life too. Many of us have encountered times where fewer new people are joining our churches and fewer still are becoming Christians, where the enthusiasm of members dials back a little, where new initiatives struggle to pick up momentum and where it feels like you are in a rut.

Jonathan saw the predicament that the people were in and he took it seriously. There are few things that drain faith from the people of God quicker than inertia, particularly when it seems like even the leaders have no compelling faith or narrative of what

God is doing. When you are stuck, your number one priority must be to somehow get unstuck. For Jonathan, this meant going on a little adventure. When nothing is happening in your church, sometimes all that is needed to break the blockage is just to do something. Especially when that something is full of faith.

Jonathan turned to the young man who carried his armour and said, 'Come, let us go over to the Philistine garrison on the other side' (1 Samuel 14:1). This was a small and easily actionable step. He didn't even tell Saul, he just did it. If Jonathan had wanted to do something on a bigger scale, it would have probably needed to go through Saul and others first, and there is a good chance it would have been held up in the inertia that was already present. Taking this small step was the best way for Jonathan to get things moving again.

Momentum is a funny thing. Often when we are stuck, we can feel like we need to do something big in order to turn things around: a building project; sending out fifty people to start a new church plant; opening a café. These are all good things to do, but they are much more likely to succeed if you already have the winds of momentum at your back than as a way of trying to get something happening. It is much better to start small if you are feeling stuck. Pioneer a new group with just one or two faith-filled people and grow it out. Find some low-hanging fruit and go for whatever wins you can see. If there are things that you can do that have very little downside but the potential for a decent gain, these are great things to go for at this stage.

Initially, when Jonathan and the armour bearer set out on their adventure, they didn't know whether God was going to do something through it or not. This is reflected in the way Jonathan pitched the mission to the armour bearer: 'It may be that the Lord will work for us' (1 Samuel 14:6). He didn't know for sure, but there was a chance that God might work through their efforts, so they gave it a try. This is the heart of the Have a Go Culture.

We see something similar as the book of Acts tells the story of the spread of Christianity in the few decades following the death and resurrection of Jesus. Empowered by the Holy Spirit, the apostles preached the good news of the gospel and started churches in town after town throughout the Mediterranean region. What is particularly interesting is that not every town saw the same level of success, nor were they planned to the same degree of detail. In some places, they were responding to the guidance of God as to where they should go, in other places they were implementing a strategic plan, and sometimes they just responded to the opportunities in front on them. Guided by the general instruction to make disciples to the ends of the earth, they seemed very ready to take a shot at whatever opportunities came their way, knowing that sometimes it would work well, and other times less so.

Part of the reason that our churches can get stuck today is our tendency to wait for too much certainty before we are willing to act. We often look for multiple prophetic words from distinct and reliable sources, coupled with a strategic plan and set of resources (money, people, etc.) that can handle any eventuality. Prophetic words and strategic plans are good, but there is also a place sometimes for just stepping out in faith with one or two others, having a go at something and seeing if God is in it as you go.

Whilst you may not know what God is doing when you set out, you do want to discern as early as possible whether this particular venture is God's will or not. If it is, then you can ramp up the resources that you are throwing into it, and if not there is no harm in bringing it to an end and investing your efforts somewhere else. In order to do this, Jonathan suggested a test. As they showed themselves to the Philistines, if they were invited up then they would interpret this as a sign that God would come through for them. God gave them that sign and so they knew that they were not in it alone, and their faith was significantly strengthened by this knowledge. Asking for this kind of sign may not always be the best way to discern God's will (though I have known many situations where God speaks through such things), but looking to God to speak in the early days of a new adventure is crucial, particularly if you are stepping out in the 'have a go' spirit without receiving a direct word from the Lord.

A Have a Go Culture and Certainty

Saying 'let's have a go and see what happens' can sound as though it lacks faith, particularly when you think of the heroes of Hebrews 11, whose faith operated as an assurance of what was not seen. And yet I believe the contrary is true. Because God has made promises regarding the future, and because we can hold those promises with the absolute certainty of faith, this gives us the freedom and confidence to try things in the present that we do not have certainty about, in the knowledge that they may be the things that God uses to bring his certain promises to pass.

As a church leader and planter, I am always interested to see how Jesus instructed his disciples regarding his mission. In *Jesus and the Victory of God*, N.T. Wright says, 'The evidence points, I suggest, towards Jesus intending to establish, and indeed succeeding in establishing, what we might call cells of followers'.[6] As we have seen, Jesus did this from the very start when, after having a great impact in Capernaum and seeing many people healed, he chose to move on to the next village rather than address the growing crowds. Then we saw how Jesus was filled with compassion for all the people of Israel, so he prayed a mighty prayer for workers and sent out the twelve in pairs to multiply his ministry.

In this season, we see the parallel tracks of 'certainty' and 'have a go' working together. Jesus commissioned the disciples with authority to cast out demons, heal the sick and preach the kingdom of God. Simple, right? There seems to be a certainty that these things would happen. How it would work out in practice at each new village they encountered was less certain. In fact, Jesus knew that unless they 'had a go' they would not know what the outcome would be. He gave them two very different ways of handling what could happen. On the one hand, if they were received and welcomed by a person positively, they should stay with that person and start building a community of peace (Luke 10:6-7). They should eat what was put before them and recognise this as part of God's provision for them. On the other hand, they might not receive such a positive reaction and in this case their response was to be very different (Luke 10:10-11). Jesus wanted the disciples to see that not every place where they tried to get a community planted would work out. In fact, they might experience a hostile reception, and being able to handle this was part of the disciples' learning curve. Jesus wanted his followers to think about building a kingdom movement and not just get stuck in the first place they happened to have a bit of success.

Working out these two principles of being certain in faith and having a go has been a key ingredient to the success of our time in Manchester. We truly believe that Jesus has promised to build his church, and we see no reason why we wouldn't see the outworking of this in our city, and yet we know that this promise can't be directly applied into every new initiative we start. But rather, we have a go, look for God in it and trust in him with certain faith that he will use whatever he chooses to fulfil those promises.

A Have a Go Culture and Fun

I am a firm believer that church should be fun (I would be reluctant to join one that wasn't), and in my experience the two things that create this sense of fun are the camaraderie of close friendships with others and the sense of stepping out on an adventure for God's kingdom. The Have a Go Culture engages people in both of these ways as it invites us to step out together and make a difference.

I believe this is also the key to enabling people to grow spiritually. Maturity comes not only by knowing the truth but by putting it into practice. As I have stepped out over the years and taken risks, I have learned a lot about myself and have begun to understand the difference between faith and presumption. Even when things didn't go to plan, the friendships formed, the lessons learned and the laughs shared along the way made the experience of trying worthwhile and left us the better for it.

A Have a Go Culture and Risk

We talk about pioneering and adventure a lot, and it would be easy to conclude that we take a lot of risks. I am not so sure this is the case. We have learned that it is possible to take big risks in a low risk way. I am always looking to ventures that have a big potential upside and a small potential downside.

On one occasion I remember a conversation with another movement leader, where I shared with him that we were looking at planting a church with a young, single guy. His response was to ask, 'Isn't that a massive risk?' Around the same time, I was helping one of the churches that I serve find a new leader for its congregation of nearly 200 people. I explained that it was a much bigger risk to appoint a new leader of 200 people than it was to start a new plant with a single guy. If the new church didn't take off then it would only affect one person, who as a minimum could learn some lessons and emerge stronger from the experience, whereas if we picked the wrong leader for the more established church then 200 people could suffer. Sometimes risk just comes down to perspective.

I do believe it is possible to minimise risk, and this is part of why we plant new sites using the four-step process that I outlined in chapter 4. Initially we make a big noise about it, trying to recruit an initial team. At this stage the risk is low, and if it doesn't generate interest then so be it. Just like Jonathan and the armour bearer, we are stepping forward and trying to figure out whether God is in it. Once we have recruited a few pioneers, the next step is a midweek meeting. Again, we are keeping our eye on how the group grows and trying to see whether Sundays look viable. If it doesn't take off then there is no harm in regrouping and trying again somewhere else. By the time we launch Sundays we know that the risk factor has increased. If it doesn't work from here then it is more likely that people will get hurt in the process, so we want to be pretty clear before we do this that God is in it, and we throw at it whatever resources we need to in order to make it work. By building step by step in this way, we are able to manage a big risk by splitting it into several lower risk steps.

The other side of this approach of taking lots of low risk steps is that we have become very comfortable with failure. Of course, we want everything that we do to work, but we won't allow that desire to hold us back from trying new and uncertain things. There are plenty of things that we have tried to do that haven't gone as we had hoped, but by developing the culture of always stepping out and seeing what happens, we have found a way to keep the risks low whilst the potential gains remain high. This has been instrumental to our growth in Manchester.

I am aware that it is a lot easier to write about failure than it is to live it out. When we do decide that an initiative hasn't worked out, our first priority as leaders is to help those involved in the project to understand that the failure is not a reflection on how much God loves them, or on their abilities; it may simply be a good idea that was actioned at the wrong time. Ending something is not an easy call to make and it requires real wisdom. We pray hard about when we should pull the plug on something and when we should persevere and battle through.

A Have a Go Culture and Momentum

For Jonathan and his armour bearer, the adventure paid dividends. Initially it was tough, and they had to fight hard for their first successes. The so-called adventure with God at this stage amounted to little more than scrambling up a hill on all fours. It wasn't easy and it wasn't glamorous. Stepping out with God rarely is. As they scaled the hillside, Jonathan and the armour bearer were fighting with the enemy combatants that they encountered, and they were able to kill around twenty men. The first twenty were hard work, and the two young warriors had to exert particular effort to defeat each one.

Once Jonathan and the armour bearer had managed to defeat the first twenty of their enemies, everything changed. There was panic amongst the Philistines, and their large army started to scatter. The Israelite army noticed what was happening and got involved in the battle, and they won a great victory that day. The enemy was defeated. All the people were mobilised. God was glorified. All because of the spirit of adventure in two young men who decided to step out and have a go, and see what God wanted to do with it.

The same can be true for our churches and plants. As we step out in faith and attempt some great adventures for the sake of the gospel, with the attitude of 'who knows, maybe God will do something', then there will be victories to be won, and these victories will mean that people get saved, communities get transformed, and the church that had previously been stuck gets re-energised and has some fresh momentum, and develops fresh faith for the adventure ahead.

Chapter Seven:
A Think the Best
Culture

As I look back on my life and leadership, one of the people who has influenced me more than any other is Terry Virgo, the founder of Newfrontiers. Over the years, Terry and I have become very good friends, and this friendship started when I was a young up-and-coming leader in my church. Even though I didn't always handle myself in the most mature of ways and had a habit of saying stupid things, Terry saw something in me and fought my corner to be brought into leadership. Before long, Terry had invited me onto his Newfrontiers international leadership team, where I had the privilege of serving with him for many years.

As I look back, I see that Terry thought the best of me, and in doing so he created an environment that allowed me to prosper, grow and rise to a level of leadership that I could only dream of. In a lot of ways, Terry's approach to me reminds me of the approach that Jesus took with his disciples. Jesus would frequently associate with tax collectors, lepers, 'sinners' and others whom it would be easy to write off and think the worst of. Whilst Jesus did not deny the very real flaws that the person had, he did not focus on these flaws, nor did he allow the flaws to come to define the person. Rather, Jesus saw past the flaws to the person, created in God's image, and he enjoyed spending time with that person and had faith for what they could become. I love this attitude; it has become the foundation of how I treat others around me, and part of the culture of our church.

A Think the Best Culture and Expectation

Of all of the disciples of Jesus, it is the story of Matthew that I think best shows the Think the Best Culture in action. When Jesus first found Matthew, he was sitting at a tax collector's booth. As a tax collector, Matthew was not a popular man. He collected tolls for the occupying Roman Empire, and was therefore both a collaborator and an extortionist. If Jesus had been looking for a reason to disqualify Matthew, then it would not have been hard to find.

Sadly, this is exactly the premise from which many church leaders begin. I can think of lots of conversations that I have had with leaders who can find a reason why pretty much everybody they can think of shouldn't take on responsibility. This is an overly conservative approach that begins with the notion that people need to prove their worth or maturity before they can do anything. Such an approach can feel like we are waiting for those serving with us to let us down, and it stifles the growth and development of people. It's as though we are waiting for pre-packaged leaders to just turn up out of the blue rather than seeing and developing the potential in the people that we already have.

Andrew Carnegie was an American industrialist in the nineteenth century. John Maxwell tells the story of one occasion where Carnegie was being interviewed, and the reporter shared the statistic that Carnegie had forty-three millionaires working for him. He asked him how he had managed to recruit that many millionaires into his business. Carnegie replied that these men had not been millionaires when they had started working for him, they had become millionaires as a result. Carnegie went on to explain how he was able to develop people so effectively:

> Men are developed the same way gold is mined. Several tons of dirt must be moved to get an ounce of gold… but you don't go into a mine looking for dirt, you go looking for gold. That's exactly the way to develop positive people. Look for the gold, not the dirt; the good, not the bad. The more positive qualities you look for, the more you are going to find.

Theologically, we know it is true that in each of us is dirt and in each of us there is gold. The first word that God spoke over humankind is, 'it is very good'. We have fallen and tarnished that goodness with sin. We are in God's image but that image is broken. There is gold and there is dirt. The bottom line is that whichever of these things we look for, we will find.

If we go looking for dirt in a person's life and then use what we find as a reason to erase their name from consideration as a leader to develop, then we will end up with a very short list and very few leaders. Bad choices, poor performance and moral mistakes can cause us to write off a potential leader. But all of these things were true at times of Jesus' disciples (including Matthew), and yet these men were never written off. On the other hand, if we look for gold we will find it. We will see the gifts of God in the lives of people, and can help develop that gold so that the dirt is brushed away and the gold shines through.

When Jesus met Matthew, he looked past the dirt and found a man who had the faith to take him at his word, the commitment to walk away from a job that he would never be able to return to if it didn't work out and the generosity to throw a great party for his friends (and Jesus). This is just what happened when Terry

Virgo saw me, and looked past the dirt that others noticed to see gold. It has also happened countless times since as we have built churches and movements with leaders that were unproven and had rough edges, but that God was at work in. It all starts with seeing the gold in someone and having faith for what God can do in their life.

A Think the Best Culture and Honour

What most offended some of Jesus' contemporaries about his interactions with Matthew was that he was willing to share the dinner table with somebody who was, in their eyes, not worthy. And to make matters worse, lots of other unsavoury characters were there as well. We are told in Matthew's gospel that once Matthew had left his booth, he went back to his house with Jesus to eat. 'And as Jesus reclined at table in the house, behold, many tax collectors and sinners came and were reclining with Jesus and his disciples' (Matthew 9:10).

In the culture of the day, a meal was much more than a bite to eat. When you ate with somebody, you were treating them as a brother or sister, and were bestowing dignity upon them. And this is exactly what Jesus was doing with Matthew and his friends. According to Joachim Jeremias, 'to invite a man to a meal was an honour... it was an offer of peace, trust, brotherhood and forgiveness.'[8] People were offended, because Jesus extended honour to those who were deemed unworthy.

Honour sits right at the heart of the Think the Best Culture, and we must treat everybody with dignity, respect and love. This is something that Paul emphasises in his letter to the Corinthians when he speaks about the church as the body of Christ:

the parts of the body that seem to be weaker are indispensable, and on those parts of the body that we think less honourable we bestow the greater honour, and our unpresentable parts are treated with greater modesty, which our more presentable parts do not require. But God has so composed the body, giving greater honour to the part that lacked it, that there may be no division in the body, but that the members may have the same care for one another. If one member suffers, all suffer together; if one member is honoured, all rejoice together. (1 Cor. 12:22-26)

We have found that eating with somebody is still a great way of showing them honour (I will talk about this more in the chapter on the Good Food Culture), and we are very deliberate in opening our homes and tables up to one another, and being sure to include people who would otherwise be excluded. One of my elders, who is based in a poorer part of town, recently invited a couple of new guys to the church to join him for a McDonalds after the service, and they were visibly very moved to be invited – they went on to tell him that nobody had ever invited them for food before. Our elder gave these men dignity and honour as he extended the invitation, just as Jesus honoured Matthew by joining him to eat.

Sharing food with people is part of what honouring them involves, but there are other things too: Taking time to talk to people, even when it is hard work or emotionally draining; giving people opportunities to participate in the life of the church; and sending an out-of-the-blue text message to see how they are doing. These can all contribute to honouring a person, as can many other things. It comes down to treating people like people, and applying the Golden Rule of 'whatever you wish others would do to you, do also to them' (Matthew 7:12), even to those who others might look down on.

A Think the Best Culture and Discipleship

Perhaps the reason that some leaders have low expectations of their people and struggle to see the best in them is that it is sometimes hard *not* to see their sinful behaviours and immaturity. Some parts of the body really do seem 'weaker' than the others, and the gold in them might be obscured by the 'dirt' that is at the surface. The idea of the Think the Best Culture isn't to pretend that those issues don't exist, but rather to have faith in the power of God to bring change and growth in that person, and to see who they can be in the future.

When Jesus called Matthew to follow him in Matthew 9, the idea wasn't that Matthew would stay as he was, but rather that he would learn and grow as a disciple of Jesus. Matthew immediately became part of a learning community, and in just the short space of time that spans the rest of the chapter, Matthew saw Jesus raise a girl from the dead, heal a bleeding woman, open the eyes of two blind men, cast out a demon, preach in many towns and heal many diseases. This is very different from the classroom-based approach to training that is common today. Matthew grew and developed by being part of a community that learned ministry from seeing and participating in what Jesus did. The best context to develop new leaders is to invite them to be with you in the things you are already doing and train them on the job.

Hot on the heels of this experience in Jesus' training community, at the beginning of Matthew chapter 10, Jesus gives Matthew (along with the other disciples) authority to heal diseases and cast out evil spirits, and he sends them out to do the very things that he himself has been doing. The instruction was to go from village to village, staying if there was a welcome and leaving if not. It was quite possible that Matthew would spend time ministering in a number of villages before he next touched base with Jesus. Jesus' way of giving Matthew ministry was characterised by high trust and low control. After a relatively short time of learning from Jesus, he was given responsibility and trusted to complete his ministry without micromanagement. Potential leaders are choked when too much control is exerted over them, but are empowered when they are given space to lead.

It seems as though Jesus had a very low bar for Matthew: he was able to get started and take responsibility straight away, without having much of a track record and whilst still having issues to work through. It also seems like Jesus had a very high bar for him, as he saw all that Matthew could be and set to work helping him to develop and grow and bring the gold to the fore.

This idea of a low bar and high bar is one that I have adopted as I raise up leaders in our church (I have already alluded to it in the chapter about the Second Chance Culture). Put simply, I want to see everybody involved in the life of the church and I want everybody to be able to influence who we are and where we are going. This means that I want everybody serving, so I need to make sure that the bar is low enough that this can happen!

Because I am not just planting a single church but starting a movement, I want to bring through loads of new preachers, worship leaders and elders. I know that doing so will mean that I can't always go with seasoned leaders, and will need to raise people up in-house that are thus far unproven. Over the last two years we have trained approximately 100 new preachers (around half of them have had the opportunity to preach on a Sunday) and we are always looking for people to whom we can give the opportunity to lead worship, run a small group or pioneer a new site plant. Often I make this call based more on potential than maturity.

This doesn't mean that we ignore issues that we can see in somebody's life. I care deeply about people's personal growth, their walk with God, their private Bible reading, their prayer life, the way they conduct their relationships, their financial management, and so on. Growing as a disciple is very important. But the low bar means that we are thinking the best of them; we are giving them an opportunity, and with it hope for the future. When I read the gospel accounts of how Jesus trained up his disciples, it seems that he gave them opportunities to take responsibility concurrently with the challenges that he brought to their character. He didn't wait for them to reach a certain level of maturity before they shared in his ministry, but both God's work in them and God's work through them were part of the process from day one.

One of our sites was led by a guy in his late twenties. Until he and his family relocated last year, he had been with CCM for about five years. I remember roughly two years into his time with us, he said to me, 'Colin, at my old church all they would let me and my friend do was greet on the door and occasionally play drums – but you have got us running a congregation!' It would be unfair on the person in question to suggest that this is an example of the 'low bar', as he is a very godly and gifted man who did an excellent job. However, it does very nicely highlight the idea of allowing people to step up and play their part who might be overlooked by others.

A Think the Best Culture and Hope

If the low bar means that we give people opportunity, the high bar means that once somebody has that opportunity we expect them to grow, and we help them to mature into the role. Again, I think back to Jesus and Matthew and I notice the faith that Jesus had for him. Jesus saw somebody who could minister the kingdom, preach the gospel and heal the sick even before Matthew saw it in himself.

Maxwell once said, 'Anyone can see people as they are. It takes a leader to see what they can become, encourage them to grow in that direction, and believe that they will do it. People always grow towards a leader's expectations.'[9] The high bar is about seeing what somebody can become and encouraging them in that direction. Jesus had high expectations of what Matthew could become. Matthew grew to fulfil those expectations, and ended up named as an apostle, a key leader in the early church and even a New Testament author!

If we are going to develop the ability to see past what somebody is to what they can become, then we need to be on our guard against the cynicism that is prevalent in our society (particularly in the UK, where I am based). Cynicism can be defined as 'an inclination to question whether something will happen or whether it is worthwhile'.[10] When this attitude is applied to the work of God in somebody's life, it is deadly. How can you think the best for somebody when your default mindset is to assume the worst? Cynicism must be banished from our hearts and our churches. This is not just a cultural point but a theological one. When we are born again and receive the Holy Spirit, something radical has happened to us. As the apostle John wrote, 'You, dear children, are from God and have overcome them, because the one who is in you is greater than the one who is in the world' (1 John 4:4, NIV). This means that the cynicism of our society is replaced by hope in God, and hope in God means that, by his power, every one of us can change and can thrive. If God is at work in a believer then surely we must trust in his power at work in their life and think the best of them. When we talk about helping people through pastoral situations or developing new leaders, this must be our starting position: think the best.

This is not to say that it is always plain sailing. Even after Jesus had seen the best in Matthew, there were plenty of moments where he was far from a perfect disciple. On one occasion, a man asked him to heal a boy with seizures, but Matthew was unable to do it. Another time, he was caught bickering with the other disciples about which of them was most important. When Jesus was arrested and crucified, Matthew ran away.

There were numerous times that Matthew messed up. Some of them were character issues, whilst others were ministry failures. As we develop people, we will come up against both, and in my experience, a culture that wants the best for everybody provides fertile ground for challenging people's behaviour and seeing real change in their lives. I have found that most believers want to have feedback, and are open to being challenged about areas of sin in their life or situations that they handled with immaturity.

We want to build a church where we make disciples who are making disciples, and helping them address each other is an important skill. Sometimes people come to me with concerns about the lifestyle choices of somebody else. This is an opportunity to see the best in both parties and to build culture. For example, when somebody raised a question about somebody else's drinking habits, it opened up a conversation about where they found the information, their own attitude to alcohol and whether they have talked to the person in question about the issue. This meant I could coach the person who had come to me in how to think the best of the person they were talking about, and at the same time in how to help them to grow. Sometimes the real issue may be what is presented, but other times there may be something else behind it, or even a particularly legalistic approach from the person raising the issue.

I want to give people tools so that they can know how and when to address people. Doing this in the right way is so important in establishing the Think the Best Culture, and doing it badly could easily undermine what we are trying to build. I am a firm believer in praying and (where possible) waiting for the right opportunity, where a natural door is opened to the corrective conversation that eases the way and gives a restorative flavour to what is said.

There will always be setbacks in the process of developing people, and moments where challenge is required, but we shouldn't see these setbacks as the end of the road. Jesus did not allow the setbacks to derail Matthew's potential. When he got it wrong, he got a second chance. When he got it wrong again, there was a third chance. And then a fourth. Everybody makes mistakes. The question is whether we are willing to give those leaders we are developing the opportunity to bounce back, learn from the mistake and come out stronger, just like Jesus did for Matthew. We have found at Christ Church Manchester that as we think the best of people, and give them second chances as necessary, they have tended to step up to those expectations and do very well indeed.

Chapter Eight:
A Generous Culture

In the law of Deuteronomy, Moses commanded the people not to be 'hard-hearted or tight-fisted' towards a poor brother or sister, but rather be 'open-handed' and freely lend whatever they need (Deuteronomy 15:7-8, NIV). The visual image of a tightly closed fist contrasted with that of an openhand presents a powerful illustration of what generosity looks like in our lives and in our churches.

Generosity is an amazing virtue that has an almost unparalleled power to change the atmosphere in a group of people. Let's be honest: having a night out with a tight-fisted person can be a draining experience. There they are, sitting in the corner with a diet lemonade that they have been nursing for hours, and notable by their absence when it comes time to buy a round of drinks. It is so much more enjoyable to be in the company of somebody who is generous, and when a whole group is full of generous people then you are well set to have a great time with each other!

Kind, liberal, big-hearted and open-handed are all descriptions of a generous person, and this is at the heart of another key strand of the culture that we are building at Christ Church Manchester: the Generous Culture. This is reflected in the early Jerusalem church, where we are told that 'all who believed were together and had all things in common. And they were selling their possessions and belongings and distributing the proceeds to all, as any had need. And day by day, attending the temple together and breaking bread in their homes, they received their food with glad and generous hearts' (Acts 2:44-46).

The Message paraphrase of Proverbs 11:24 reads, 'The world of the generous gets larger and larger; the world of the stingy gets smaller and smaller'. We have certainly found this to be true in our experience at CCM; the more we have leaned into our Generous Culture, the more opportunity and influence we have seen coming our way.

A Generous Culture and Poor People

Right at the top of the agenda when it comes to a Generous Culture is generosity towards poor people. This is a strong apostolic foundation in our movement, and one that we wholeheartedly embrace. Remembering poor people is a theme that is brought repeatedly in the Scriptures. As I have already alluded to, Moses commands the people in Deuteronomy, 'You shall open wide your hand to your brother, to the needy and to the poor, in your land' (Deut. 15:11). The prophet Isaiah had a word for a people who were diligent and sincere in their religious practice and yet ignored poor people. He said, 'Is not this the fast that I choose: to loose the bonds of wickedness, to undo the straps of the yoke…? Is it not to share your bread with the hungry and bring the homeless poor into your house?' (Isa. 58:6-7). Jesus himself said, 'when you give a feast, invite the poor, the crippled, the lame, the blind, and you will be blessed, because they cannot repay you' (Luke 14:13-14).

We see this lived out in the early church. We are told in Acts 4 that in the early Jerusalem church, 'no one said that any of the things that belonged to him was his own, but they had everything in common' (Acts 4:32). The astonishing result of this Generous Culture was that poverty was completely eradicated within this church community. We are told in Acts 4:34 that 'There was not a needy person among them, for as many as were owners of lands or houses sold them and brought the proceeds of what was sold and laid it at the apostles' feet, and it was distributed to each as any had need'.

The priority of poor people has many expressions in our church. It starts with building people who care, and who have a habit of meeting needs as they see them, in organic and low-profile ways. From an organisational perspective, we set aside a budget line dedicated to helping individuals in our midst with needs that arise, following the lead of the early Jerusalem church. In addition, we partner with other organisations that are able to provide a level of specialist expertise for the needy that is beyond what we can offer. One of our sites is in Gorton, which is a community in the top 1% for deprivation in the UK. This site is well aware that it cannot meet all the needs of the community and so has developed a very close partnership with a local Christian day centre called The Oasis Centre. Through this we have seen the church play a part in serving the neediest in practical ways, and many clients of the Centre have found their way into the church and come to faith in Christ.

Perhaps the biggest expression of our Generous Culture towards poor people is our special Give Big Sunday offering. Every year we have two such special offerings, in May and November, and the November one is always dedicated to poor people. Not a single penny goes into the running of the church, but it is all given away. We have found that this offering never fails to lift the hearts of our people, and last year we were able to give away the equivalent of more than two months' regular church giving to poor people.

When we give this money away, we want to make sure that we are blessing those outside the church as well as in. The Roman Emperor Julian once complained that the Christians of his time 'care not only for their own poor but for ours as well'. We want to embody this same spirit. Recently Andy Burnham was elected as the first mayor of Greater Manchester. As one of his first priorities he launched a fund designed to eliminate homelessness in the city, and personally committed 15% of his own salary to the fund. This is a great initiative coming from the political sphere, and we are looking at different ways that we can partner with him in this project (including financial support). This sort of partnership is important on a number of levels: it demonstrates a generous spirit towards the city and its different people groups; it helps curtail a partisan spirit; and it feeds into the ideas of building an open-handed people.

A Generous Culture and Resourcing

For me, one of the most important moments in developing a Generous Culture at CCM came a couple of years ago in a conversation with some of my key leaders about a new school of theology that we were planning to develop. The idea was to provide highquality theological training that was accessible to people who had a full-time job and other life commitments. We came up with a model that was based on scheduling one Saturday morning per month for two years, bringing in the best Bible teachers and theologians we could to provide this training. When we ran the numbers on this idea, it turned out that such a course would end up costing us a lot of money, and so we started talking about how much we wanted to charge people to access the course.

Around this time, one of our sites was in the middle of a teaching series that was helping people with their financial management. This series was built around the outstanding Making Change series that was put together by Craig Groeschel.[12] In one of his talks, Groeschel shares about how his church was just beginning to grow in influence at a time when they were stretched financially and struggling with debt. Because of the attention they were getting, lots of people were asking about purchasing their resources, and this could have turned out to be quite a lucrative way to ease their financial pressures. As Groeschel tells the story, somebody on the team asked, 'What if we give the resources away?' Despite being a scary move and a step of faith, they knew it was the right thing to do and have since given away millions of free downloads.

We found this story inspiring and it caused us to think of our school of theology in a new light. Talking about a Generous Culture in church has to mean more than just getting people to give us lots of money! This was the moment to literally put our money where our mouth is, and so we have chosen to make the theology course completely free, whilst keeping the standard high. We get to put on something that will bless many people, and to do so without financially burdening them.

We have taken a similar approach in other ministries that serve the wider church. A few years ago we set up Broadcast, an online training hub designed to support, train and encourage church planters and other leaders.[13] In the early days of this we dabbled with the idea of charging people a fee to access some of the training, with the idea that the ministry could become self-supporting. There was something about doing this that never really sat right in our guts, and we quickly realised that we should change the model and make the resources free, treating Broadcast as our gift to the wider church.

We are not dogmatic about this point, and understand that there are reasons that certain resources need to come at a price, particularly in-person training that requires overnight accommodation and/or travel. But where possible, we want to apply a Generous Culture to the way we resource the wider church and offer as much as we can either free of charge or at an accessibly low price.

A Generous Culture and Planting

It is impossible to overstate how crucial generosity is to multiplanting. Without a Generous Culture, it would quickly grind to a halt and nothing else would get started. Whenever a new site is pioneered, there are things that it needs in order to get up and running. It spends more money than it brings in. It needs an influx of passionate and gifted people to get it going. It often then needs to 'rent a crowd' until it gets more established. It needs to be splashed around with a bit of profile, crowding out the air-time for other things.

All of these needs must be met from somewhere, and this somewhere is usually the other sites. If the new site is a net drain on the budget, this can only work because the other sites give more to the kitty than they spend. If the new site needs people to get going, at least the first few of these come from existing sites (and often a few more end up gravitating that way in time as they find the new location more convenient for where they live). If the new site rents a crowd, they rent it from other existing sites, and the profile that the new site gets is usually at the expense of a lower profile for the other sites. In short, starting a new site means that all of the other sites take a bit of a hit.

This means that attitude is everything. It may be possible to get a congregation or leader to support a new site begrudgingly once, but to repeatedly support new planting with people, money, prayers and goodwill requires a remarkable generosity of spirit. Over the years as we have started new sites, I have been so encouraged to see the amazing sacrificial generosity of our church, and it causes me to value all the more the Generous Culture that we have built.

A Generous Culture and Hospitality

When we think of generosity, our minds probably go initially to money, but there is much more to the Generous Culture than just the financial element. One of the most important ways that generosity shows itself in our church is through hospitality. As people first encounter the church, the way they are greeted, hosted and generally cared for will speak volumes about the values of the church. Jesus was once hosted by a religious leader named Simon, when the meal was interrupted by a lady who performed some rather unconventional acts, causing the host to complain to Jesus about her actions. Jesus said to Simon, 'Do you see this woman? I entered your house; you gave me no water for my feet, but she has wet my feet with her tears and wiped them with her hair. You gave me no kiss, but from the time I came in she has not ceased to kiss my feet. You did not anoint my head with oil, but she has anointed my feet with ointment.' (Luke 7:44-46). Simon failed to show the hospitality that a host would have been expected to show a guest in his home in that culture, showing not even basic care, let alone generosity.

Generous hospitality is important in how we use our own homes (we discuss this in more detail in the chapter on having a Good Food Culture) but also in our gathered meetings. Having plenty of food and good quality tea and coffee at the beginning and end of church meetings again demonstrates generosity. Sometimes churches can struggle with this because of the time commitment it involves, in addition to the financial cost, but for us it is something we have made a priority in both our Sunday services and other church meetings. The Bible lists hospitality as a quality that is required of an elder, and we tend to apply this to their home life, but I wonder if we should also apply it to the meeting that they oversee.

A Generous Culture and Giving

I have no doubt at all that we have got as far as we have in Manchester because of the incredible generosity shown by lots of people, some of whom don't have much to give at all. The first site that we started is in one of the very poorest areas of the city – far from the ideal location to unlock funding for more planting – and yet this site bankrolled the next plant into studentland. At the same time, some key members of this site caught a vision for poor people in India and were able to raise a significant amount of money for this work. I find it incredibly inspiring when people who don't have very much themselves choose to give what they do have to advance God's purposes. It reminds me of the story that Jesus told of the widow who gave her last mite into the temple offering.

As we have grown and more sites have been started, we have tried to keep something of this generous approach to giving, and we are constantly surprised at how much is given by students, those on lower incomes, and also those who have a bit more and choose to approach it with open-handed generosity. Every year we budget in faith for an increase in income, and every year we have seen giving increase to meet the needs. We are very blessed to have such a financially generous church!

In addition, we have seen the Generous Culture expressed as people give significant amounts of time to their ministry. Most of our staff members are part-time, often sacrificing better remunerated jobs in order to serve the church. In addition, we have dozens of incredibly gifted volunteers who are diligently serving alongside day jobs and family commitments, and their generosity with their time inspires us all to generosity with our own.

A Generous Culture and Faith

The way we approach our church budget leads nicely on to the final point about the Generous Culture: that it is fuelled by faith in God's provision. God himself is rich in generosity, and we see this in so many ways; not least the glorious world he has created for our enjoyment and the incredible cost he paid for our redemption. In addition to this, we are promised in several scriptures that God will provide for our needs, including Philippians 4:19: 'And my God will supply every need of yours according to his riches in glory in Christ Jesus'.

God's abundant generosity provides fuel for ours. Not only is it an example to follow, but it is an assurance that resources are not scarce, and we do not need to adopt a mentality that holds tightly to what we have; rather, faith in God's fatherly provision will lead us to share what we have and generously put others before ourselves. Indeed, Jesus himself said, 'give, and it will be given to you. Good measure, pressed down, shaken together, running over, will be put into your lap. *For with the measure you use it will be measured back to you*' (Luke 6:38, emphasis added).

Rather than causing us to worry that giving will leave us with nothing, Jesus promises that, as we give to others, more will be given to us, and this has certainly been true in our experience. Whilst some 'prosperity preachers' may have abused this idea to extract money from people, it really is a precious truth that inspires generosity coupled with faith in God's providing hand. And it links back to the idea that we started with, that 'The world of the generous gets larger and larger; the world of the stingy gets smaller and smaller'.

Chapter Nine:
A Forward Looking
Culture

I have had the privilege of sitting with many church leadership teams over forty years of ministry. During this time, I have noticed that there are some common (unhealthy) ways of thinking that exist in small churches and large churches alike. One in particular often shows its head when a church is considering embarking on some new initiative, only for somebody on the team to suggest, 'Let's wait until we have more people or resources and do it then'. On the surface, this way of thinking seems sensible. More people usually means more skills and gifting, and therefore the church's capacity to try new things increases. Right? More resources means you can pay for the initiatives that you are suggesting. That makes sense, right? I don't think so. At the risk of sounding a bit over-dramatic, I would suggest that this kind of thinking is a cul-de-sac from which there is no escape.

The challenge for a larger church (whatever that means in your context) is that it can become a little bit like an elephant. You need to feed the beast more and more just to keep it alive, leaving fewer people and resources for new initiatives. Often churches will say that they are (or that they aspire to be) a 'large resource church', when in truth they are channelling proportionally fewer people and resources into initiatives that serve the wider church, poor people and church planting.

Smaller churches can also get stuck in the 'not until we have more people' mindset. When your church is just a few dozen people, your volunteer base is pushed to the limit. Everybody is on PA, kids work and welcome, and everybody is a little tired, so any new people or resources that come into the church tend to be deployed to make life a bit easier. Again, this seems logical, but it may be another cul-de-sac from which it is difficult to escape.

In his book, *The Multiplying Church*, Bob Roberts puts it this way:

> Some pastors believe they cannot start a [new] church until they first grow their [current] church to a large size and make [it] debt-free. Some will say they are waiting until their church gets 'healthy' – and that is defined in so many ways. Those who say, 'we are not big enough yet', especially when they have a hundred people, don't have an accurate definition of the church.[14]

The simple fact is that we want to see Jesus' kingdom expand. I am sure that no church leader would disagree with that statement. We all want to see people saved and added, poor people lifted up and society changed. In more basic terms, we want to see the churches that we lead grow in both depth and breadth and be instrumental in seeing many new churches, sites and kingdom initiatives started. To do this you must dig into your church's culture. Are you truly forward looking in your approach? Are your people? At Christ Church Manchester we have worked hard to build a Forward Looking Culture into the church.

A Forward Looking Culture and Growth

The first component to grasp of the Forward Looking Culture is the expectation that growth is the normal state of affairs. Jesus compared his kingdom to a mustard seed; it starts small but it gradually and steadily grows until eventually it becomes a large and mighty tree. Growth is normal.

We once ran a preaching series where we allowed people to submit their big questions about Christianity online and then took a few weeks to respond to some of the questions in our sermons. One of the questions that we addressed was, 'Why do we not see the same kind of growth and miracles today that happened in the book of Acts?' This is a question that many of us would resonate with: of course we all read the biblical accounts of remarkable moves of God's power and long for this to be our daily experience.

When we think in this way it can be easy to underestimate what God is doing in our own day, and perhaps to overestimate what happened in Acts. We should remember that the book of Acts actually tells a story that spanned over about thirty years. Whilst we might read it a chapter per day, we should realise that this is not the speed at which growth took place. The remarkable moments (such as 3,000 people being saved on the day of Pentecost) were punctuated with steady growth (people being added daily). If this daily growth was, say, two people per day on average, then the early Jerusalem church grew by a rate of around 20% per year: a fairly similar rate to the average growth that we have seen at Christ Church Manchester in the decade since we launched the church. And of course, we are far from being the only church out there. Globally, statistics indicate that on average over 58,000 people give their lives to Jesus every single day.[15] This is almost twenty times the scale of what happened on the day of Pentecost, and corresponds to the equivalent of a Pentecost-sized salvation every seventy-five minutes!

This is similar with church planting. In Acts we track the missionary journeys of Paul, who would go to a city and spend a couple of years getting a church planted before moving on to the next place and leaving that church to take responsibility for reaching its region. We think of ourselves in a similar way to one of those churches that Paul started, and have operated at a fairly similar pace to him: we tend to start a new church or site every one to two years. Again, as we look at global church planting we see a pace of kingdom advance that far surpasses what happened in the book of Acts. God is not slowing down in our age.

Don't mishear me on this point: if the church that you lead is not growing at the moment, this is in no way meant to condemn or discourage you. There are various reasons why this may be the case, and it is important to develop an understanding of what some of these reasons are in your context. Hopefully though, understanding the growth dynamic of God's kingdom will give you hope that your current plateau need not be permanent, as well as steadfastness to keep pressing on for breakthrough, and expectation of what God can do through you.

A Forward Looking Culture and Change

Of all of the aspects of the culture of Christ Church Manchester, the Forward Looking Culture is one that takes the greatest level of leadership intentionality to keep alive and strong. It takes a degree of bravery to keep asking 'what's next?', particularly when your current position is already stretched! Andy Stanley writes:

> Leaders provide a mental picture of a preferred future and then ask people to follow them there. Leaders require those around them to abandon the known and embrace the unknown – with no guarantee of success. As leaders we are asking men and women not only to follow us to a place where they have never been before; we are asking them to follow us to a place we have never been before either. That takes guts. That takes nerve. That takes courage. We all know the fear associated with walking into a dark room or traversing an unlit path. Leading into the future conjures up many of the same feelings.[16]

I agree with him completely. Many times I have found myself wondering whether the latest plant is a step too far or whether I should ease up a little to give everyone a break. Whenever I feel like this, I re-read the Gospel of Mark!

When I look at the ministry of Jesus, I see that it always had a forward thrust. Jesus came to preach the gospel of the kingdom, and he wanted to bring this message to every village in Israel in a time frame of just three years. This motivated him to make some critical forwardlooking decisions.

As I discussed in chapter 2, at the start of his ministry, Jesus quickly gathered a crowd in Capernaum, and Peter – like so many leaders – wanted to consolidate this advance and stay where he was. Jesus disagreed, and said, 'We must go on to other towns as well, and I will preach to them, too. That is why I came' (Mark 1:38, NLT). Later, with the task of getting to every village far from complete, Jesus instructed his disciples to pray for the Lord to send new workers into the harvest field. He followed up this prayer request with the bold move of splitting up his apostolic team into six mission bands, then sent them out to different villages in his name. As if this were not enough, Jesus then followed this up by sending out seventy-two others, adding thirty-six new teams. From these, I believe Jesus gives us some clear keys to show how we can plant and have faith for the next thing, whilst still working on the current one.

I often wonder what the twelve disciples thought when Jesus picked out seventy-two others to go and start new communities. We will never know, as their response was not recorded, but I do know that in many churches that suggest a new church plant, site or other kingdom initiative, some of the first reactions will focus more on what the existing community will lose by sending – and this is often quickly followed by a statement about the supposed lack of maturity of those who could go and plant. For Jesus, the mission was so important that he needed to press on to what was ahead, and was willing to do so with disciples who were still a work in progress, knowing that they would grow and mature as they played their part in kingdom activity.

As one leader once said, 'The task of leadership is to make the status quo more dangerous than launching into the unknown'.[17] Jesus could not settle for the status quo because he knew there were eternal consequences if things stayed as they were. Compassion for the multitudes of Israel made him launch the twelve and then the seventy-two into the unknown. Anger at the exploitation of poor people and those who had travelled to the temple from other nations motivated him to clean the traders out of the temple. And he wept as he raised Lazarus from the grave, demonstrating that death would be defeated.

Getting everything clear, organised and well-ordered before embarking on the next thing may sound like a sensible approach, but it is not always possible, and will often slow progress and leave us stuck in the status quo. I believe that the mission is way too important for that!

A Forward Looking Culture and Resources

At the heart of the objection to new initiatives that I opened this chapter with is the issue of resources. Few of us feel like we are in a place where we have the money to spare or the qualified people to start something new, especially when we are looking to plant churches or sites into expensive urban centres or deprived communities. This is a real challenge, and one that we should engage with seriously.

When Jesus sent out the disciples in pairs, he kept things simple and had the expectation that the pioneering teams would travel light, would have a simple strategy to gather, and would live by faith. As he sent them, his instruction was, 'Do not get any gold or silver or copper to take with you in your belts – no bag for the journey or extra shirt or sandals or a staff' (Matthew 10:9-10, NIV). It seems that Jesus expected that part of the team's contribution to the overall mission would be faith for provision, and that new people would also contribute resources.

We have tried to apply something of this principle to our planting in Manchester and have developed an approach to pioneering that keeps costs low and faith high! Our plants start out very lean, usually in a home or a free public space, and the leader at this stage is usually a volunteer. Even when we go to a public Sunday meeting, we are looking for a room with a capacity of sixty to ninety people, and have found that such rooms tend to be in fairly ample supply and reasonably priced. We keep the PA and tech so compact that it can be stored under somebody's stairs and fit in the boot of a car. By this stage we are looking to pay somebody to lead this site, but this will just be one or two days per week and they will supplement it with work elsewhere.

Because we are always looking to do the next thing, we can sometimes be thought of as a risk-taking church, but this is not an accurate description of the way we work. Ninety percent of the forward steps that we take have a very low potential downside. We don't commit too many financial or personnel resources at the earliest stages, and it is only as these initiatives gain traction and show evidence that God is in them that we then increase our investment.

Every once in a while, however, a church that is looking forward will need to do something that seems riskier and to 'bet the farm' in pursuit of something that God is calling them into. This has only happened once at Christ Church Manchester, and it proved to be a pivotal moment for us. At the time we had just one site, with around fifty people meeting in the outer suburbs of east Manchester, and we had the opportunity of hiring Tim Simmonds to pioneer our second site into the student district of Manchester. Paying a year's salary for Tim on top of our existing budget was going to take all of the church's savings, and yet we were convinced that this was the right move. We made it very clear to the church and to Tim that this was a big risk and that we could only afford a one-year contract.

This was a risk that we needed to take, and it was the beginning of a season that propelled us from being a struggling church that was going nowhere fast into the beginnings of an exciting multisite church. As it turned out, at the end of that year we still had all the money left in the bank that we started with, and we were able to keep Tim working for us (though he did need to go part-time – students don't transform the balance sheet overnight!). The crowd of young people that Tim was able to gather gave us a huge injection of energy, talent and amazing zeal for God. That big risk taken by fifty people turned into six Sunday meetings in five sites and over 300 people – and the journey is only just getting started. The decision was not taken lightly, and we may not do anything like it again, but we bet the whole farm on that one.

A Forward Looking Culture and Innovation

Part of embracing a Forward Looking Culture is about embracing new ideas, methodologies and technologies. It is interesting to look at the missionary methods of Paul and notice how he was able to leverage the system of Roman roads (the new technology of his day) to facilitate the advance of the mission. We have looked to do something similar.

Having a good digital presence is a fairly obvious application of this (though it amazes me how dated some church websites seem). We work very hard on our website and social media presence; and we have had lots of people visiting and joining us who have found us this way.

We have also worked hard on innovation in other areas. The musical styles in our meetings have developed greatly, and we have tried lots of different things here. We have pioneered global community groups via Skype as pastoral support for students who are with us on years abroad. We have also innovated a bespoke church financial management system that meets the unique needs of a multiplanting church. These are just a few examples, and we are constantly looking to both innovate new ideas and adopt good ones that we hear about that haven't yet caught on elsewhere.

In 1962, Everett Rogers conducted a study into how new ideas and innovations catch on. This study has received a lot of attention in the last couple of decades, and was referenced in Malcolm Gladwell's book, *The Tipping Point*.[18] Rogers concluded that there are five separate segments of the population that interact differently with any new innovation, as shown in the diagram.

diffusion of innovation curve

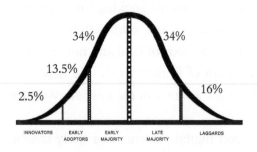

Source: Four Norweigen Zero Emission Pilot Buildings: Buildings Process and User Evalution. Available from: https://www.researchgate.net/figure/The-Diffusion-of-Innovation-Curve-Rogers-1962_fig2_322337558 [accessed 19 Dec. 2018]

A minority of the population (2.5%) can genuinely be classed as *innovators*. These are creatives and creators who make things happen out of nothing and are overflowing with ideas that have never been thought of before (2.5% equates to one person in forty, so there will probably be people like this in your church; try to creative an environment for them to thrive). Then there are the *early adopters* (13.5%). They pick up ideas and fashions from the innovators and jump on board before they go mainstream. They are at the front edge of most new fashions and lead the way for others to follow. Then come the *early majority* (34%) and the *late majority* (34%), who follow the crowd once the innovation has caught on, and finally the *laggards* (16%) who may never adopt the new idea. As leaders, it is important to think about where our church is positioned on this curve. As a forwardthinking church, it is important that we innovate and adopt early, and by the time a good idea moves from early to mid-adopters, we want to be all over it.

A good example of this is Broadcast, the church planting training ministry that we set up a few years ago. The problem that we were trying to solve was providing some community and training support for people planting churches, which can often be difficult to access because planters are out on a limb in remote contexts. About this time, Google had launched its Hangouts app, allowing up to ten people to be on a video call together, which could be recorded and streamed to YouTube. At the time, we had never heard of anyone using it in a church context, other than for a one-on-one call, but we had a hunch that it could be used for our purpose, so we got a few planters that we know onto a call and booked in an experienced planter to teach them for half an hour and take some questions.

When we started, we didn't necessarily have a grand vision for what Broadcast could become; we had just spotted a new piece of technology that could solve a problem that we saw, and we had a go. Over the years we have refined and developed Broadcast, and what we do with it now is much better than what it started as. Now there are lots of people using Google Hangouts or similar platforms in this kind of way. If we had waited until we had a perfect plan to get started, the window of opportunity to do something that few others were doing would have closed. By being an early adopter on this new platform, and iterating as we went, we were able to ride the front of a new wave and innovate a great new way of serving remote church planters.

A Forward Looking Culture and the Past

One of the biggest challenges for a church that wants to look and move forward is getting a right relationship with the past. It is important to honour those who have gone before and whose faithful sacrifice and pioneering in their own day have helped you get where you are today. Looking forward in no way disrespects the past, and if anything it honours it by building on the foundation that has been laid and reaching for new horizons. In my experience, there are two major ways that the past can hinder progress in the future. Both past defeats and past triumph can stall future advance if we don't know how to move beyond them.

In order to deal with past defeats, we need to deal honestly with the disappointments that they have caused. It says in Proverbs 13:12 that 'hope deferred makes the heart sick', and this can often prevent people from wanting to step out again, and even turn them into critics of those who do want to. Helping people to identify what is going on in their hearts and why they have become scared of stepping out in faith is a big part of developing a Forward Looking Culture.

It is equally important that we leave behind past triumphs. Whilst we should enjoy reaping the fruit of what we have sown in the past, it is important not to let the forms and methodologies that have served us well blind us to where God is leading us today. Too many churches have worship services straight out of the 1990s and sermons straight out of the nineteenth century. Even if what we are doing is contemporary for the people we are reaching today, in a few years' time it will no longer be so, and we must be ready to do new things and respond to a new move of God to reach a new culture with the only thing that will never change – the gospel of Jesus Christ.

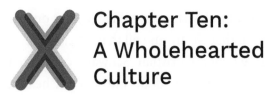

Chapter Ten: A Wholehearted Culture

Of all the characteristics of worship that he encountered, the one that seemed to please Jesus most was worship which came from the heart. One time, Jesus noted the financial gift that a destitute widow made to the temple when she chose to give away her last couple of pennies, and he was more moved by this than by the larger gifts of others who had money to spare. The widow was all in, and Jesus commended her for it.

When it comes to the people serving in our church, I feel the same way. There is nothing that thrills me more than seeing people giving their all for God's kingdom with a smile on their face and eagerness in their heart. I remember last year arriving at a Saturday morning baptism service with crowds of others, to be greeted by a team of enthusiastic bright students who were among the first to arrive and the last to leave. As well as serving in Sunday meetings, they had given up their Saturday to set up, to prepare food, to wash dishes and to greet people, and they did it with care, joyful laughter and contagious enthusiasm. This epitomises what we are building at Christ Church Manchester, and is something that we have come to call the Wholehearted Culture.

A Wholehearted Culture and Worship

Being wholehearted begins with the way we treat Jesus himself. Just as the woman in the gospels poured out a jar of perfume worth a fortune, so we want to lavish everything we have on our saviour. He is worthy of all that we are and all that we can give.

In the 1990s, the researcher Christian Schwarz conducted the most comprehensive survey ever done into church health, speaking to millions of people in dozens of countries. Schwarz boiled down the characteristics shared by healthy and growing churches into a few key characteristics. It should come as no surprise that Schwarz concluded that churches do well when the people are passionate about living for Jesus. He writes, 'The point separating growing and non-growing churches, those which were qualitatively above or below average, is not style at all. Instead it's this: Are Christians in this church on fire? Do they live committed lives and practice their faith with joy and enthusiasm?'[19]

Schwarz calls this characteristic 'passionate spirituality', which is a good way of articulating what we are getting at when we talk about a Wholehearted Culture, and we see it lived out as we look at the life of the early Jerusalem church. The people there were devoted to the apostles' teaching, fellowship, breaking of bread and prayer, they were filled with *awe* and they ate together with *glad and generous hearts* (Acts 2).

Wholehearted worship of Jesus must find its expression in our gathered worship times. There must be the expectation that we will meet with God during these times. Of course, any believer has access to God all the time, and yet there is something particularly precious about the times that we come together as a people to worship. These times are nothing less than being awakened to the presence of God himself, and so we engage with our whole being. Worship is not a spectator sport, and in our meetings we create settings that make it easy for people to get involved and bring their worship. In part, this happens by planting meetings of a size that makes it hard to get lost in the crowd, by teaching into how the Holy Spirit leads the church in its worship through the different gifts outlined in the later chapters of 1 Corinthians and other passages, and by keeping a listening ear for the promptings of the Spirit as we lead meetings and following in the direction that he guides. In a large part, building a culture of wholehearted worship is also done by modelling, and as people see their leaders fully engaged in worship, singing with passion and gusto and a smile on their face, raising their hands, kneeling before God and pouring out their heart in praise, this becomes contagious and the culture is caught much more than it could ever be taught.

It is also worth at this point making a note of how we can encourage engagement within a meeting itself. We were recently visited by Simon Brading, a worship leader from Emmanuel Church, Brighton, who also leads at NewDay (a Newfrontiers youth event). He led a training session on Worshipping in Spirit and Truth.[20] Simon noted that he has seen lots of people who were leading worship or leading a meeting try to draw people in with words like, 'Come on now, let's all really worship with all that we have.' He pointed out that whilst the heart behind this kind of call to worship is good, it is based on law; people will be worshipping simply because we are telling them to. Instead, he suggested drawing people into worship with the gospel. Share a couple of verses packed with truth about who God is and what he has done for us, and capture our hearts afresh with such glorious truth that the only possible response is wholehearted praise. I must say that I have found that the truth of God's gospel has a power to lift hearts and change the dynamic in a room way more than even the best music ever can.

Wholehearted worship also finds expression when we are not together. In Romans 12:1 Paul says, 'present your bodies as a living sacrifice, holy and acceptable to God, which is your spiritual worship'. Our gatherings may be an important part of our worship, but so too are the rest of our lives. We are to consider ourselves as living sacrifices, and doing so means that we must follow Christ in a wholehearted manner. In chapter 7 I spoke about the low bar that we have for getting people started in ministry. Along with this low bar comes a very high bar for the vision we have for what our lives of devotion and obedience can become; that the kind of disciples we are building are ones who will love the Lord with all of their heart, all of their soul, all of their mind and all of their strength, and who will love their neighbour as themselves.

A Wholehearted Culture and Volunteers

Another key area in which the Wholehearted Culture manifests itself is in the attitude of volunteers. When commitment is willingly given, and hard work is undertaken with joy and passion, this is a wonderful thing. As we nurture this culture, we must give careful thought to how we recruit and motivate our volunteers. Approaching it with the grace and love of Christ is the foundation of building a wholehearted attitude within our volunteers. Sometimes churches can feel the pressure of gaps in a rota and so strong-arm somebody into filling the gap or give a desperate notice in a Sunday meeting that highlights the need. We have found that when recruiting is based around guilt or legalism, it rarely produces the kind of enthusiastic, joyful volunteers that we are looking for.

As I think back to the volunteers at the baptism service that I spoke of above, they were a mix of students who had been with us for a few years, who had grasped the culture and felt comfortable in the role, and of others who were a lot newer. As the latter saw the fun that the others had while serving, and the playful spirit on the team, and the dedication to the task, they were drawn in and threw themselves into the role with a much greater enthusiasm than would ever have happened if they had been recruited through obligation or guilt. The Wholehearted Culture is contagious, and there is nothing quite like serving alongside passionate people to encourage your spirit and renew your own commitment to serve.

Jesus trained his disciples in how to go about recruiting volunteers when he sent them out. He instructed them to pray for the Lord to send workers into the harvest fields – which were plentiful – then he sent them out themselves. Whatever the size of the church, it always seems that workers are in short supply. However, having a leader who has the faith to pray for new workers, and the willingness to personally invite the right people into the role, makes such a difference.

As Paul spoke of the Philippian church, he called them 'partners in the gospel', Thinking of those who volunteer in our churches in this way honours the role they are playing and inspires commitment. Understanding that they are a stakeholder who has a role to play in making decisions in church life serves to motivate people. In my view, one of the mistakes that many multisite churches make is centralising too many decisions and so disenfranchising people who are serving at site level. We try to leave as many decisions in the hands of our site as possible, and draw lots of stakeholders into this decision-making process.

Being wholehearted is the not the same as being intense. When done well, it will make serving a lot of fun for those who volunteer. When people are naturally smiling as they serve, we know that we have got something right. It is important to us that we care well for those who are serving in the church, and enjoy lots of laughs and good food together as we do so.

A Wholehearted Culture and Excellence

One of the values that is often spoken about in church leadership circles is 'excellence'. I must confess that I have mixed feelings about this. On the one hand I am very sympathetic to the idea. Nobody likes a sloppy approach, and I have seen Sunday meetings and other aspects of church life done badly in so many places that I can see the appeal of a real focus on quality. However, I think there is a dark side to excellence, and I am not convinced that a church culture built around excellence is always a particularly healthy place to be.

When I hear the word 'excellence', it brings to mind the idea of reaching a particular standard of performance, and this doesn't chime well with what I read in the New Testament. When Jesus commends the widow for her offering, what she brought was significantly inferior to what the wealthier people around her brought, and yet because it was all that she had and she brought it with faith and radical generosity, it was her gift that Jesus commended rather than theirs. She may not have been able to attain to a particular standard of excellence (depending, of course, on how exactly you define the word) but she was able to bring wholehearted devotion, and this pleases Jesus far more than the larger gift.

When I invited my friend Steve Boon, who manages a large multisite church in Brighton, to spend a couple of days helping us to think through the infrastructure of Christ Church Manchester, Steve used a phrase that has been very helpful as we have thought about the interplay between excellence and wholeheartedness: 'Good enough is good enough'. Striving for perfection will knock the wind out of a Wholehearted Culture. By setting a bar that is unattainable for 90% of volunteers and driving hard for that standard, you end up disenfranchising your people and demotivating those who are working hard. The result is often that good people gradually drift away from your serving teams, or even from your church altogether. Far better that people do their absolute best without the pressure of some arbitrary standard of 'excellence' hanging over them.

A good example of this is in the training and development of new preachers. When somebody is learning their craft, the end result may not be excellent from day one, but if they have worked hard, been teachable, made progress and thrown their heart and soul into it, then I am very happy with what they have done and will look to give them more opportunities. The final sermon may not be on the level of Tim Keller, but it is usually a solid exposition of a Bible passage with some decent application thrown in, and at this stage in their development I think that is good enough. Good enough, when it comes from a place of wholehearted effort, is good enough for me!

On the other hand, there can be times when a more experienced and gifted preacher gives a sermon that is objectively much better than the one preached by the rookie, but they have coasted in their preparation and relied on their eloquence and charisma without really seeking God, deeply engaging with the text or working hard on their presentation. I can understand that there may be situations where emergencies arise and this kind of rushed preparation is the only option, but when this becomes a pattern for somebody it is a much bigger problem in my eyes than the new preacher who gives their all and preaches sermons that are 'good enough'. Wholeheartedness is far more important to me than excellence (and wholehearted people tend to be motivated to work on their craft and will end up reaching an 'excellent' standard anyway).

Excellence doesn't come for free, and when the price of excellence is empowerment, this is, in my mind, too great a price to pay. The paradox in bringing through new leaders and delegating responsibilities, is that it will almost inevitably mean that the task is done less well after it has been delegated than it was before, at least for a season. The trick is to hold your nerve during this time as the person you have brought through learns, grows into the role and develops their own approach. In the end, the task will probably be done at least as well as it was before delegation, often better, but it takes a while to get to this point. It is time well spent.

In my experience, one of the things that keeps wholehearted people passionate and thriving in their gifting is helping them get some wins. When people are given opportunities to do things that matter, that are within their abilities and that they can see the results of, it causes a hunger for more. Jesus did this with his disciples. Very early on he gave them the responsibility of baptising new converts. When 5,000 people needed feeding, Jesus managed the situation so that it was the disciples who actually fed them. It is important that we draw people into tasks that matter, and give them the support that will enable them to succeed and experience wins. Even when it is obvious that somebody is in a role that just isn't a good fit for their gifts, we want to find a way to let them transition out of the role with their head held high and with the confidence to take on other roles in the future.

Another factor in this is trust. Genuinely delegating not just a task but the authority that goes along with it, and resisting the temptation to jump back in at the first sign of trouble, is a practice that needs to be developed in the church. I have found that delegating in a way that is marked by low levels of control but high levels of accountability creates an environment in which people thrive and engage wholeheartedly.

A Wholehearted Culture and Honour

One of the key dynamics in a Wholehearted Culture is honour. People quickly disengage in an environment where they feel unappreciated or unnoticed, or if there is a dynamic where leaders lay heavy burdens on the people and treat them as problems to be solved rather than as partners in Christ. As we think about, pray for and address the church, some of the terms that we should major on include 'people of destiny', 'world changers' and 'God's treasured people'. Enabling people to see that they are caught up in God's cosmic mission puts their contribution into its true eternal context. Having a belief that God's kingdom will triumph, and letting this hope and optimism shape our practice, motivates and energises people. As we speak destiny into people, particularly the destiny that is promised to all believers in Christ, we see them respond with wholehearted devotion.

It is important as we honour people in the church for what they do, that we don't limit it to those in prominent public roles. I love it when I enter our Sunday meetings and am greeted enthusiastically. Seeing plenty of cakes and fruit and drinks makes me a happy man, and it is a priority for me to thank and honour the people who make these things happen, both on a personal level as I express my appreciation individually, and by publicly thanking them on a suitable occasion.

One component of honour is encouragement. This was such a priority in the early church that one of the key leaders was nicknamed Barnabas, meaning 'The Son of Encouragement'. Wholehearted people are nourished in an atmosphere of encouragement, which brings out the very best in them and enables them to reach higher.

Another component of honour that shouldn't be overlooked is partying. On my fiftieth birthday, the church that I was leading at the time organised a surprise hog roast for me. I loved it, and the care that was shown in planning the event and the number of people attending made it all the more special to me. A hog roast may not be right for everyone, but finding contexts to celebrate with people and party together beyond the ministry tasks that we share in honours them in a deeply personal way and affirms them as friends and brothers and sisters in Christ. And it forges bonds that will strengthen the ministry and increase the heart-level engagement!

Chapter Eleven:
A Good Food Culture

I can clearly remember the first Alpha Course that I attended. We would meet together weekly to discuss the gospel, pray for people and enjoy a meal together. One of the things that most struck me was how instrumental the food was in helping people to relax, make friends and get some great conversations flowing.

Once Alpha was finished, we returned to our regular midweek groups, which often used an icebreaker that felt awkward and slightly forced to try to get people talking. I couldn't help but think that we were missing the natural conversation that flowed around the table at Alpha. As I reflected on these thoughts in light of the Bible, I began to realise that our Alpha Course was a much closer reflection of what gatherings looked like in the New Testament than many church home groups were!

It is surprising how many of the best-loved stories about Jesus happened over food and drink. There is the Last Supper, and the time when Jesus fed over five thousand people with just five loaves and two fish (plus another time when he did similarly for four thousand people!). Jesus was a guest at the wedding in Cana where he saved the day when they ran out of wine, and he partied with disreputable people like Matthew and his friends. He was repeatedly eating at the homes of the Pharisees, and when he picked out Zacchaeus and spoke words of acceptance and salvation to him, he did so by inviting himself to dinner at Zacchaeus' house! Following his resurrection, Jesus spoke with two of his followers on the road to Emmaus; they didn't realise it was him until he sat down with them and broke bread, and at that moment their eyes were opened. When Jesus forgave Peter for his betrayal, he did so by sharing a barbecued breakfast with him on the beach. Jesus apparently saw eating with others as a big part of his ministry, and in Luke 7:34, he even says of himself that, 'The Son of Man has come eating and drinking'. As Robert Karris writes, 'In Luke's gospel, Jesus is either going to a meal, at a meal or coming from a meal'.[21]

Food and drink also feature heavily in the picture the Bible paints of the future. When Jesus spoke of the coming kingdom, one of the key images that he chose was that of a great wedding banquet, resplendent with good food and fine wine. This kind of language echoes Isaiah, who writes of that day: 'On this mountain the LORD of hosts will make for all peoples a feast of rich food, a feast of well-aged wine, of rich food full of marrow, of aged wine well refined' (Isaiah 25:6).

As I think back to that Alpha Course in light of the emphasis the Bible places on food, I begin to understand why the meal is such a powerful part of the evening. It has also made me consider the way I think about small groups in church life. There have been times in the past where I have heard complaints from group leaders that they only get full attendance when there is food on offer. It would be easy to assume that the issue to solve here is one of commitment, and that may be part of it, but it may also reflect the beauty of the biblical way of sharing life around the table. I know that I am more excited to go to a meeting if food will be a part of it. Perhaps the best answer to this problem is simply to eat together more often. As a church we try to do as much as we can together over food and drink, and the term that we have used for this is the Good Food Culture.

A Good Food Culture and Hospitality

It may sound simplistic, but we have found that one of the best ways to start and grow a new church is by having people round for dinner as often as possible. A few years ago, we had started a new site and the couple who were leading it were looking to me for a bit of advice. I told them to put on a good meeting every Sunday morning and then open up their home and have a load of people round for lunch each week. It worked, and the community they were planting grew quickly. I am convinced that without this priority of eating together and forging community, things would have gone a lot slower for them.

In the New Testament we are told about the early believers: 'breaking bread in their homes, they received their food with glad and generous hearts' (Acts 2:46). It seems that eating together was the norm for them, and it is for us too. I have heard it said that the two key ingredients in loving relationships being formed are shared food and shared laughter. In my experience, there is a lot of truth in this. At CCM, we try to have food together in as many of our community groups as we can and there are often meals at or after our Sunday meetings. That said, hospitality cannot be entirely programmed, and I love to see the spontaneous hospitality at work in our church as people are very generous in opening their homes and hosting meals for others.

Creating a culture of hospitality, like any culture, takes both time and intentionality. I used to think that this was mainly a challenge to us in the UK, but I once had the audacity to preach on this theme in India, and one of the leaders in the church that I was speaking at confessed to me that he felt very challenged by what I had said. He told me that because hospitality was such a priority in his culture, it had become competitive, and they had backed off from inviting others round for food because they couldn't compete with what some other people were serving. I think this is a temptation for people in any culture. When we go to a 'special effort' to offer an elaborate meal in a spotless house to our guests, we may feel like we are honouring them, but in truth we are raising the bar of hospitality to a level that is intimidating for many and we are placing an artificial barrier between our guest and our normal life. True hospitality involves treating people like family and inviting them to share in our everyday lives – messy house, ordinary meals and all!

Hospitality can sometimes feel like hard work, but it is a crucial part of building church. Peter encourages his readers to 'show hospitality to one another without grumbling' (1 Pet. 4:9). As the costs of hospitality start to have an effect on your money, your time and your opportunities to hunker down with your family, it can be the source of a lot of pressure in life. It can sometimes feel easier not to bother, or at least to grumble about it a little, but Peter encourages us to keep going and continue showing hospitality to one another in a cheerful manner.

A Good Food Culture and Outsiders

In addition to the hospitality that Peter urges us to show to 'one another', there is hospitality shown to outsiders. In fact, the Greek word for hospitality is *philoxenia*, which literally means 'love for strangers'. The Good Food Culture that we are building at CCM is not one that is inward looking but that looks to draw other people in and share the blessing.

Caring for and welcoming guests is an important part of being a hospitable church. There is nothing worse for a new person at church than standing on their own waiting for somebody to come and talk to them. It becomes more awkward the longer we make them wait! At CCM we have built a culture where people are quick to introduce themselves to newcomers and make them feel welcome, and it is not unusual for a first-time visitor to be invited for coffee or meals by several people over their first week or two in the church. When this happens, it doesn't take long at all for them to feel like they are right at the heart of the church community.

I mentioned earlier the importance that the Bible places on food, particularly in terms of the coming kingdom. Instead of seeing food as a secondary feature of our gatherings, we must view it as a part of the new age of God's kingdom. Wright highlights this in *Jesus and the Victory of God,* along with the stunning implication of whom Jesus chose to share table fellowship with: 'Most writers now agree that eating with sinners was one of the most characteristic and striking marks of Jesus' regular activity. Jesus was, as it were, celebrating the Messianic banquet, and doing it with all the wrong people.'[22]

When the church gets hospitality right, it has a powerful impact on a world that is largely disconnected. Henri Nouwen wrote:

In our world full of strangers, estranged from their own past, culture and country, from their neighbours, friends and family, from their deepest self and their God, we witness a painful search for a hospitable place where life can be lived without fear and where community can be found. Although many, we might even say most, strangers in this world become easily the victim of fearful hostility, it is possible for men and women and obligatory for Christians to offer an open and hospitable space where strangers can cast off their strangeness and become our fellow human beings.[23]

This movement from hostility to hospitality is full of challenges. Our society can be suspicious of those who reach out in kindness, and anxious about making themselves vulnerable as they build relationships with new people. Yet our vocation as God's people is to convert the stranger into a friend, and to create the kind of free and fearless space in which it is easy to get to know the community and become part of the family.

The writer of the Hebrews gives an incredible incentive as he urges the church to show hospitality to outsiders: 'Do not neglect to show hospitality to strangers, for thereby some have entertained angels unawares' (Hebrews 13:2). I do wonder as we grow our sites and have tons of people back to our homes after our Sunday meetings each week, whether we have yet had any angels at our tables!

A Good Food Culture and Gatherings

Being intentional about the Good Food Culture in the church means that we need to carry this value through every area of church life. Every time we have an elders' meeting we start by sharing a curry. Our community groups find ways of eating together: sometimes it's just puddings, other times it's a BBQ.

One of our sites has a monthly midweek community meal where they all come together to eat and invite lots of others from the surrounding area. Another site eats Sunday lunch together, either in their meeting venue or in people's homes. Yet another site kicks off their Sunday services with sausage or bacon butties. The exact menu is not prescribed centrally, but the priority of good food in our Sunday meetings runs through everything we do.

The kind of refreshments that we offer in our Sunday meetings is a big deal for me. I remember reading Nelson Searcy's book *Maximise*, where he uses the illustration of a church that offered doughnuts to guests but first cut them into quarters to keep costs down.[24] I believe we can do better than that and should show generous hospitality to anyone who walk through the doors. Cheap biscuits and instant coffee send a very clear message to people, and it is not a good one.

Sometimes I have joked that good coffee is more important in a new site than a good leader! I wouldn't quite go that far, but I do insist that a nice coffee machine is one of the first things that we buy at every site, and I am convinced that there is a correlation between good coffee and church growth – even if I don't yet have the data to prove it!

I should also point out at this stage that offering good food in our Sunday meetings means that we think about what will bless all the different types of people attending. Our minds may initially go towards snacks like doughnuts and pastries, and there is certainly a place for these, but we have found a lot of people in our meeting appreciate it when we also offer a range of quality fruit. We also try where we can to make gluten- and dairy-free options available. Most people with these dietary requirements don't necessarily expect to be provided for in church refreshments, but it is a wonderful opportunity to surprise and delight people and show that you are thinking of them. When somebody sees that you have anticipated their needs and care about providing for them, they are a lot more likely to stick around with you for the long haul.

A Good Food Culture and Contextualisation

Showing hospitality is an important part of church in any culture; so much so that it is listed in the Bible as a prerequisite for an elder. That said, as we have planted into some very different parts of Manchester we have learned that the form of hospitality that best serves the people in one community will vary greatly from that which suits those in the next. In some of the poorer communities of Manchester, being invited into a stranger's home for food is not the done thing and serves to alienate rather than include, whereas in a more middle class community this would seem way more normal. This isn't to say that we give up on hospitality in these communities, but simply that we find other ways to express it that are a better cultural fit. The key to contextualised hospitality lies in finding an appropriate safe space in which hospitality can be given and received.

It is important in gathered hospitality settings to be mindful of those who are not financially well off. Paul rebuked the Corinthians because, as they shared a communion meal together, the richer members of the church arrived early and ate all of the food, leaving nothing for those who were poorer. It would be unhelpful and potentially humiliating to draw attention to the different socioeconomic positions of those sharing the meal, but it is well advised that those who are better off go easy until it is clear that there is plenty to go around.

It is also important to contextualise hospitality to the individual who is being hospitable, where possible. Everybody needs to show some form of hospitality, and there will always be occasions where we need to operate outside our strengths or comfort zones, but in general we should be looking to free people up to express hospitality according to the way that God has wired them. For some this might mean a packed home and party feel, for others a literal 'open house' with people coming round at their leisure. For still others it might mean intentionally showing hospitality to one or two at a time. There has to be grace for people to express the Good Food Culture in their own way.

Another part of hospitality that requires sensitivity in different contexts is that which we receive from other people. It can be viewed in many parts of the world as disrespectful and dishonouring to people if we reject the hospitality that they offer us. When Jesus sent out the seventy-two, his instruction was to find a person of peace and to stay at their house, 'eating and drinking what they provide'. When we are guests in somebody's house we should eat whatever is put before us (all the while having grace for people who can't do this for whatever reason).

Whilst we want to eat whatever we are served in the homes of others, when we are the host it is a good thing to be as accommodating as we can to the needs of our guests. Many people on my team have learned how to cook interesting vegetarian and gluten-free food so that we can be hospitable to as many people as possible.

A Good Food Culture and Good Food

You may have noticed as you read this chapter that the Good Food Culture isn't really about gourmet cuisine, but more about opening our homes and tables to one another and to outsiders, and welcoming people into fellowship over meals.

We do want to share the best of what we have, but this isn't a pressure to put on a MasterChef meal. True good food is food that facilitates community and that says, 'You are loved and you are home'. We know that we have got the Good Food Culture right when we have built a church in which everybody is welcome and everybody is fed!

Putting It into Practice

If there is one section of this book that I would hope and pray that every leader would take to heart, it is this second section where I unpack the CCM culture. The culture is the very heartbeat of what we do.

Start with Culture

I have seen people try to do church in a way that is structurally similar to what we do at CCM but that lacks the culture, and what is created can easily become toxic. If empowerment is low and control is held tightly in the hands of senior leaders, if a prohibitive barrier of excellence is insisted upon before people can take real responsibility, and if reasons are easily found to discount people from the mission, then multiplanting won't work. It will stutter and stall as soon as the capacity of one or two gifted people at the centre is exhausted.

Conversely, I know of lots of churches that come at things with a very different model or ministry philosophy from us, but that would be driven by the same cultural values. When I see a church that radiates empowering leadership, that encourages young people to have a go and take responsibility, that extends the hand of grace for the second chance, that thinks the best of everyone and that is generous with time, money, food and affirmation, it gives me great hope for what can happen in that church. Culture makes things happen.

One exercise that I would suggest in order to benefit the most from this book is to honestly evaluate the culture of your own church. Gather your team together and try to articulate some of the things that encapsulate 'how things are done around here' (and try to be honest about how things are at the moment rather than aspirational about how you would like them to be). In what ways does your church culture help or hinder your mission to reach the region that you are in?

Next think about the seven points of the CCM culture and how well they would describe how things are done in your church. To what extent do you have a Second Chance Culture when things don't go to plan? How much do you encourage people to Have a Go? Do people tend to Think the Best of one another? How Generous are people? How much of your focus is Forward Looking to what could be? How Wholehearted is your approach? How much of what you do is centred around Good Food and hospitality?

Because these cultures are about *how* things are done more than they are about *what* is done, they can make a difference right away even if you keep your programme and strategy exactly as it is. Begin to dream about how things would be different if these aspects of culture were able to permeate through your church. What are some of the first things that you can do to move in this direction?

Be warned, cultural change is not something that happens overnight. You may well reap some early benefits, but to see the real transformation that you long for is a long process, and will require your constant attention. Leadership, above all, is about shaping and managing the culture. To see these cultural changes happen, you will need first to take them to heart yourselves and live and give them your constant focus. As Tony Hsieh, the CEO of Zappos, said, 'If you get the culture right, most of the other stuff… will just take care of itself'.[6]

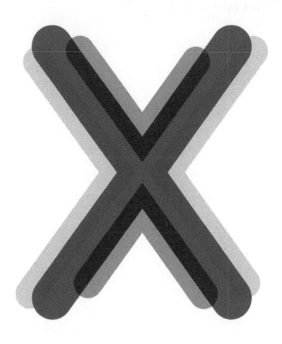

Part Three:
Multiplanting Systems

One of my favourite leaders in the Bible is Moses. Moses had the privilege of hearing God reveal his name from the burning bush. He was instrumental in confronting Pharaoh and leading the people to freedom from slavery in Egypt. He witnessed incredible miracles, and he spoke face to face with the Lord as a friend.

Leading God's people wasn't easy, and the scale of the task made it overwhelming. By the time we reach Exodus 18, Moses was stretched to breaking point. He was operating as the sole judge of the people (we can estimate from the book of Numbers that there were around 1.5 million of them) and this occupied him all day, every day from morning until evening. Clearly, this couldn't go on. Moses could not continue to operate as a visionary leader whilst taking this burden on himself.

The solution came as Moses' father-in-law, Jethro (a man who was not himself a believer), spoke into Moses' situation about the need for systems and structures. The advice was simple: Moses should appoint some judges over tens, others over fifties, others over hundreds and still others over thousands. By delegating authority in this way, Moses ensured that the people had qualified and dedicated judges to serve them, that new leaders were empowered and that he himself was freed up for other things. It is telling that in the very next chapter after Moses gave away this responsibility, he went up Sinai and met with God.

This Old Testament story foreshadows a similar incident in the New Testament. In the early days of the church there was great gospel growth, and also a lot of opposition. In Acts 6 we read of a dispute that arose over the food distribution amongst widows. This was an important thing to deal with, and yet doing so would have diverted the attention of the apostles away from the crucial priorities of preaching the gospel and prayer. What was needed was a system, so the apostles invited the church to select some capable people who could give their attention to the issue.

Both of these accounts show that for leadership in a growing organisation to work, there is a need for effective systems. Such systems don't develop on their own. Driven by some of the strategic and administrative geniuses on my team, we have developed various ways of doing things at Christ Church Manchester that have served us very well and enabled multiplanting to work on the ground.

In this final section of the book, I will share with you some of these systems and processes that we have developed. These chapters will vary greatly in content, from dealing with deep-seated principles to practical tactics that we have found to be effective. My goal is simply to give my answer to the question, 'What makes multiplanting work?'

My first response to this question isn't in a system at all, but is in recognising that it is by the grace of God that we have got as far as we have. It is only through God's presence sustaining and encouraging us, and the power of prayer changing lives, that we have made any impact at all.

After a chapter expanding this theme of prayer and presence, I will discuss some of the systems we have built for developing people. We will start with the kind of leadership that is required in a multiplanting church, then unpack how we understand discipleship and what this looks like at Christ Church Manchester. Finally we will explore why creatives have had such a crucial role in our journey and what we have done to enable and encourage this.

We then move on to explore what Sundays look like. Whilst each site has its own unique flavour, there are some key components that hold true across every Sunday service that we have. Finally I will share some of the key principles that stand behind our approach to finance and communication. These are critical elements of the life of any church, and there are some unique challenges that come with the multiplanting model. Over the years, we have built some robust mechanisms and practices that ensure we are well served in these areas.

Whilst not all of the details will necessarily transfer into a different context, in each of the chapters there are some key ideas that have provided the foundational thoughts for why we do things the way we do. These principles will provide everything you need to develop your own systems that do work in your context. Healthy systems are a must for a healthy church, and whilst they don't need to be complicated, they do need to be intentional.

Chapter Twelve:
Prayer and Presence

What makes multiplanting work so well for us? There are practical things that I have learned along the way that I will share in coming chapters. The most fundamental answer that I can give though, is that it is God who makes it work by his Holy Spirit. So the very best thing that I can do as I dream of more sites impacting more of my city is to get on my knees and pray.

Leading from God's Presence

On his last night with his disciples before he was crucified, Jesus explained to them that the key to a fruitful life is dwelling in his presence. He said, 'I am the vine; you are the branches. Whoever abides in me and I in him, he it is that bears much fruit, for apart from me you can do nothing' (John 15:5).

One of the many things that I have learned from spending decades in Newfrontiers team meetings with Terry Virgo is how essential it is to lead from the presence of God. Of course, there is a sense in which God is always present everywhere (his omnipresence) and another sense in which he has promised to be with believers always, but there are also particular moments when that presence is manifest in a special way to encourage and empower us. It is this manifest presence that the Bible is speaking of in verses such as Hebrews 10:22 ('Let us draw near with a true heart in full assurance of faith') and James 4:8 ('Draw near to God, and he will draw near to you').

This presence starts in the quiet place of personal prayer and worship. As a leader meets with God and has vibrant joy-filled encounters with him in their own devotional life, this spills over into what they are leading. Before being multiplanting leaders we are worshippers of the Most High God, and it is from this place that we are empowered for the task at hand.

God's presence isn't only where we start from, it is also where we are going and how we get there. Thinking of our Sunday gatherings, Terry Virgo once tweeted, 'If the church is the temple of the Holy Spirit, wouldn't we expect to meet him there?'[28] He is right. The very best Sunday gatherings I can remember are ones where God's presence was manifest in a tangible way, and often this means things not quite going the way that I expected. When I think about what it would look like for the communities of my city to see the kind of transformation we long for, I know that I want them to be overwhelmed with God's presence.

Stories of historical revivals inspire me and I pray for a similar outpouring in my own day where God visits us in a way that can be neither dismissed not denied.

Put simply, much more than all the tactics and systems that we could ever learn (as helpful as they can be), we need God!

Leading Through Prayer

Prayer is absolutely vital in seeing the kingdom of God advance. I know that in my own life, were it not for prayer then there is no way I would be where I am today, and the same is true for our churches. I think of the Old Testament story where Joshua is leading the people into battle down in a valley, while Moses is standing up on the hill with Aaron and Hur praying. As Moses' hands are raised, the people begin to prevail. As Moses drops his hands, they start to lose. It was through prayer that the battle was won. This is a picture of how prayer functions in our church. We still need to fight hard and do our best, and yet we recognise the pivotal role that prayer has in everything that we accomplish.

Have you ever read through the gospels looking for insights into Jesus' own devotional life? It is a fascinating exercise and there is a lot to learn about prayer by thinking about what Jesus prayed about, who he prayed with, and when he prayed.

Jesus would often pray at times when nobody else was praying. For example, in Mark 1, Jesus got up before anybody else and went to a solitary place to pray. When everybody else got up, they were worried and went out looking for him. John chapter 7 describes an exhausting day at the Feast of Booths. At the end of this day, we are told that 'they went each to his own house, but Jesus went to the Mount of Olives'. When everybody else was finished for the day and went home, Jesus was just getting started and he went to his place of intimacy with the Father. Before making key decisions like appointing the twelve, Jesus prayed all night. There are many ways of answering the question, 'What was different about Jesus?' but one of the most overlooked answers is his devotion to prayer.

In Jesus' prayers, we have a model that can guide our own prayers. When he taught his disciples the Lord's Prayer, this included the instruction to pray for very big things ('Your kingdom come, your will be done, on earth as it is in heaven') and also for the small details of what we need day by day ('Give us this day our daily bread'). Leading a church with a multiplanting model puts me firmly in both worlds; common themes of my prayers include both big picture requests, where I ask God to unlock new areas of the city, and the specific needs of the moment for our sites. 'God, give us three more drummers' is a prayer that I have found myself praying more times that I can count!

Another of the Bible prayers that I love to pray is the 'pioneers' prayer' that is found in Matthew 9:37-38. As he is going to the villages and towns of Israel, Jesus is struck by the scale of the task and is moved with compassion by the needs of the multitudes of people for gospel ministry. He points out the harvest is plentiful but the labourers are few – and as I contemplate the needs of my own city I feel a similar way! The solution that Jesus suggests to his disciples is that they pray earnestly to the Lord of the harvest to send out labourers into his harvest.

If we are going to pioneer into new communities of our cities or regions then there is a desperate need for new workers. Pray for them! Earnest prayers asking God to multiply kingdom workers are a staple part of the life of a pioneering leader. Before Hudson Taylor sent missionaries into every province of mainland China there was a moment on Brighton beach where he did business with God. With eleven untouched provinces in the nation, and a desire for a pair of workers for each, Taylor surrendered himself to God and asked him for twenty-four new workers; twenty-two for China and two more for Mongolia. It should come as no surprise that God provided the workers for the harvest field!

On one occasion I was in Uganda, helping train pastors of churches in rural villages, and I was teaching them through the book of Nehemiah. At the same time in Manchester I was trying to get a new site started in the Didsbury community and needed to find somebody who could lead it. Every time we reached part of the story where Nehemiah prayed, I stopped my teaching and asked these Ugandan pastors to cry out to God for a new worker in Didsbury. It wasn't long before we found the right person to lead it and it has grown into the Kingsway site of our church! Never be afraid to cry out to God.

The Prayer of Faith

When I pray I want to do so with faith in the promises of God. I know with absolute certainty that what God has said will come to pass, so that gives me great confidence as I echo those things back to God in prayer. In Habakkuk, God promises that 'the earth will be filled with the knowledge of the glory of the LORD as the waters cover the sea' (Hab. 2:14) and I know that includes the backwater communities of Manchester, so I pray God's promises back to him. Whenever one of our sites faces a challenge in getting established in its community, I think back to Jesus' words, 'I will build my church, and the gates of hell shall not prevail against it' (Matthew 16:18). The prayer of faith is powerful, and my faith is fuelled by God's promises.

Sometimes this faith comes mid-prayer, and I am certain that my prayer has been answered. The Holy Spirit has imparted this assurance of faith in my spirit. In 1998, Simon Pettit delivered a seminal message at the Newfrontiers leadership conference in Brighton, calling us to remember poor people.[31] I, like many other church leaders, was stirred that our churches needed to be doing more in this area, but to be honest I didn't really know where to start. So I just gathered a few other people with a similar burden, and we met weekly to pray and seek God's guidance. After a few weeks, I sensed God say that we should stop praying now because the prayer had been answered – so we did! A little while after this a new couple came along to our church. They were looking for a new church to join that had a heart for poor people, as they ran a ministry with poor people in Manchester. I was now seeing the answer to our prayer that I had known by faith a few weeks earlier! They joined our church and we were delighted to partner with them in their work.

Listening to God

A healthy prayer life is not a one-way process. As well as bringing our requests and petitions to God, we should expect to hear God speaking to us words of encouragement, challenge and guidance.

Being ready to hear and respond to prophetic input is vital for pioneering ministry. I have already shared about the time that I was picked out by a prophet who shared the picture of stakes in the ground webbed together. I wholeheartedly believe that this is from God and it has formed the foundation of the last few decades of my ministry. Quite a few members of my team have very similar stories and they are in Manchester doing what they are doing because of very specific ways that God has spoken to them.

As I need to make important decisions, listening to the voice of God is crucial. Sometimes there are things that seem logically sensible and yet God would have us go in a different direction. This was the situation for Paul in Acts 16. He wanted to go to Bithynia next to spread the gospel there, and this seemed like a reasonable plan, but the Holy Spirit gave Paul a dream specifically leading him to go to Macedonia, where he opened a door for fruitful ministry. In moments like this, it is imperative that we follow where the Spirit leads us.

A few years ago I was weighing up where we should plant next, and there were a few places that seemed like good options. Around this time a friend of mine from Coventry who didn't know that I was wrestling with this question said that God had told him that a specific part of the city would be a fulcrum for us. He had never even heard of this place, but we had. I took this word very seriously and it became the location of our fourth site!

More recently, I have been having some strategic conversations with our core team about what things I should be focussing my attention on over the next few years. There were lots of different aspects to the discussion, but the starting point was a prophetic word that I had received about a year earlier from an Indian prophet named Shjau. Listening to God's voice and making decisions accordingly is crucial.

Leading Corporate Prayer

Not long after I first moved to Manchester, I spent a weekend ministering in northern Germany. I arrived late on the Friday afternoon after a long day's travel, and I was looking forward to getting some good rest to prepare me for the activities of the weekend. When I arrived, however, I was told that the church had organised a half night of prayer and that I was expected to attend. With neither energy nor enthusiasm I attended the prayer event, and it was incredible! All through the night, intercession was mingled with worship. Prophetic songs abounded. We sang together in the Spirit and there was a wonderful sense of God's presence in the room. My tiredness was instantly overtaken by a renewed strength and energy, and from this experience, I began to understand how to sustain long and powerful times of prayer –

even with grumpy people in the room! With this as a motivation, I led our churches into a season of whole- and half-nights of prayer.

Prayer meetings are important. I always teach my team that when they are leading a prayer meeting they shouldn't leave it to the last minute, but should put as much effort and thought into it as they would a Sunday meeting. There should be worship leaders who are well-prepared, skilful in their craft, humble and worshipful in their outlook, and ready to be involved all through the evening so that sung worship can take place at any time. This doesn't happen on its own. I sometimes arrange an evening with our singers and musicians where we will sing and prophesy together and learn to flow with one another. This training is vital in preparing an environment where people will encounter the living God.

The contributions that are brought by the meeting leader or others can galvanise the prayer, or they can kill the atmosphere and make people drowsy! You want to give enough detail that people can pray in an informed manner, but it should not feel like an extended talk. This is a challenging thing to do. It requires preparation, and it is good to recognise that some people are more gifted than others at communicating in this kind of context, and to allow those people to use their gift. Whilst there is no formula to running prayer meetings, having a plan with a number of different options for how people can pray will help to keep things moving but also give you the flexibility to lead more effectively as you read the room and discern what levels of energy, faith and engagement are present.

Finally, when you are gathering people to pray, make sure that what you are asking of them is tailored to their stage of life.

Whenever you have a lot of students and young people, and also empty-nesters, you can organise meetings at fairly short notice and can pack out the calendar far more than if you have a lot of families with young children, who would be well-served by knowing what is happening as far in advance as possible, so they can make necessary childcare arrangements to be there. Understanding seasons, and planning and communicating well, play a big role in encouraging people to turn out at a prayer meeting, which in turn stirs faith and builds momentum. For many churches, thriving dynamic prayer meetings can be a challenge, but it is well worth putting in the effort. You will reap the rewards if you do.

Chapter Thirteen: Leadership

One of England's great naval heroes is Admiral Horatio Lord Nelson. He had a reputation for involving his captains in his thought process, allowing them to make decisions that mattered and trusting them to implement what had been decided. Leading in this way meant that he had officers who were loyal to him and also a community of trust amongst his key leaders.

Nelson's leadership qualities were exactly those that are required of a multiplanting leader. He was secure enough in his own position to trust others with responsibility. He was clear on his objective and decisive about the steps needed to achieve it. He was personally committed to both his mission and his strategy. Because of Nelson's outstanding leadership, an atmosphere was created in which other leaders could emerge.

Building such an atmosphere is crucial if we want to develop leaders in our churches. This is why I have spent so much time in this book explaining the CCM culture; it is these elements of our culture that have provided the fertile soil for people to grow in their character and their leadership gifting. Maxwell says, 'Those who believe in our abilities do more than stimulate us. They create an atmosphere in which it becomes easier for us to succeed. They create a climate in which potential leaders will thrive.'[33] There is much to say about the leadership skills required for multiplanting (so much, in fact, that the follow-up to this book is called 'Multiplanting Leaders'), but here I want to mention three central principles for multiplanting leaders to think about.

Multiplanting Leaders Embrace Change

Every leader is in the business of change, but this is particularly true for multiplanting leaders. After each new plant or project, there will always be voices telling you to slow down and consolidate your progress (just as Peter urged Jesus to stay put in Capernaum). As the leader, the onus is on you to keep pioneering, to initiate the next step, to make the structural changes required for further growth, to create space for the next leaders to emerge and to keep the momentum going. It is impossible to lead a multiplanting church if you are unwilling to embrace and lead people into constant change.

One of your most effective tools for leading people into change is urgency. As I mentioned in the chapter on a Forward Looking Culture (chapter 9), the task of leadership is to make remaining with the status quo more dangerous than launching into the unknown. It is impossible to change an organisation until it comes to terms with the dangers inherent in keeping things as they are. I am often invited to help leadership teams of churches that are struggling or stuck. One of the first questions that I ask is whether any of the team has experienced sleepless nights because of the situation. Unless there is this desperate urgency for change, it is very unlikely that anything will happen.

Along with an understanding of the dangers of the status quo, for change to happen there needs to be a vision for how things could be better in the future. Bill Easum explains how the ability to cast a compelling vision is crucial for leaders: 'Leaders have strong imaginations. Imagination is the ability to see clearly what doesn't yet exist and to be able to articulate it so that others see it.'[34]

The main difference between those who lead through transition and those who simply try to manage transition is the ability to articulate and communicate vision for where you are going and how it relates to where you are now. You can never talk about your vision enough, particularly during seasons of transition. It needs to be articulated in many different formats and told in ways that can capture the hearts of the whole range of people that you are leading. And through it all there must be faith, confidence and personal commitment to see it through.

Sometimes the change that you need to lead the people into is one that has a long-term vision perspective, and this type of change presents a particular challenge. It is easy to start with a flourish but find over time that the excitement about the vision is slowly fading. The best way to keep people invested is to give them short-term wins along the way. We know that sending people out to pioneer new sites will put them right on the front line of the battle, so we want to celebrate every possible victory – first small group, first ten people gathered, first salvation, first Sunday meeting, and so on – and we want to stand by their side and help resource them all we can to keep on track with these small incremental wins, because it is through these small wins that big change comes.

Multiplanting Leaders Set the Pace

The Brownlee brothers made the news in 2016, in the dramatic end to the World Triathlon Series in Mexico. Jonny Brownlee had been leading the race, which he needed to win to take the championship, and was on his final approach to the finish line when his legs started to give way. Initially he began to slow down, and then to weave all over the course, and it quickly became clear that he couldn't run anymore and would be unable to finish the race.

It was at this point that two more athletes came around the corner, who had previously been competing for second place but now had the opportunity to win. One was the South African Henri Schoeman, who went on to win, and the other was Jonny's brother Alistair. Rather than competing with Schoeman for the win, Alistair Brownlee slowed down and helped his little brother to complete the race, before eventually pushing him over the line in second place, and only then crossed the line himself to finish third.

Once the race was finished and it was clear that Jonny would be OK, Alistair was interviewed about what had happened. He said, 'I wish the flipping idiot had paced it right and crossed the finish line first. He could have jogged the last two kilometres and won the race.' This is the kind of banter that only a big brother could get away with, but it contains wisdom that is just as true for multiplanters as it is for triathletes. Pacing is crucial. As a leader, it is down to you to set the pace.

Sometimes in our planting we can make exactly the same mistake that Jonny Brownlee made, starting out with all guns blazing and then hitting a wall with nothing left to give when the key moment comes. It is also possible to make the opposite mistake and take things so slowly that momentum is never built, enthusiasm starts to wane and the window of opportunity closes before you ever get going.

A great example of this idea of pace is found in Paul's ministry in Corinth, recorded in Acts 18. When Paul first arrived he was on his own and waiting for the rest of the team to arrive. During this season, he took things fairly slowly. His main priorities were generating some finance by setting up a tent-making business, recruiting Aquila and Priscilla to be his first local team members, and spending one day a week reasoning in the synagogue as he attempted to persuade both Jews and Greeks. At CCM, we would also consider the early stages of a new site as a time to take things slowly. Other than making a bit of noise on social media, we would be keeping things low key and not throwing too much time or money at it yet, allowing a small core group to gradually emerge. Once Silas and Timothy arrived in Corinth and Paul felt he had a complete team in place, he began to increase the pace. At this point, he devoted himself to preaching the gospel. For us, this would be akin to launching a Sunday meeting, with the increased demands on time, money and focus that this brings. At this stage the congregation, and CCM as a whole, would be putting in a much more exerted effort to make the site a success. This is where pacing ourselves and going slow at the start begins to pay off.

Along the way there will be other times that you need to make decisions about pace, and this is where leaders can bring important wisdom. When somebody has ownership of a particular site, they usually want to keep the pace as high as possible, but this isn't always the right thing to do. At particular times, such as a university Freshers' Week or new site launch season, we want to have enough resources in hand to take the pace to a very high level. In order to do this well, there need to be other times when we slow things down a bit and give everyone a breather. During quiet seasons like the summer, we will often reduce the number of meetings that we run and bring a couple of sites together in the same gathering. We have also found Christmas to be a surprisingly quiet time, especially in newer sites, and so we dial down what we do at this time of year accordingly (whereas in some of the more established sites with a larger fringe we make a bigger deal of it). Healthy pace doesn't happen by accident, and one of the most significant decisions that a leader needs to make concerns when to speed things up and when to slow them down.

Multiplanting Leaders Multiply Leaders

If you are an insecure leader who needs to hold things tightly within your control, then multiplanting is not for you. At the heart of the model is empowerment, and I find myself as the senior leader often operating as a coach, spending most of my time helping younger leaders to emerge and giving them the space and guidance to operate and thrive.

When I am invited to speak with the leadership teams in different churches, one of the most common objections given when I raise the possibility of starting a new site or planting a church is that there aren't enough leaders. I believe that this is theologically wrong. It is God who gives the gift of leadership to the church, and Paul's description of the Corinthian church as 'not lacking in any spiritual gift' (1 Cor. 1:7) must equally be applied to churches today.

The main problem that we face isn't the lack of leadership gift, but the fact that it is often found camouflaged in some very unexpected places. Peter and John were described as 'unschooled, ordinary men' and Matthew was a morally suspect tax collector. Many church leaders would overlook people like this, even as they complain of having no leaders. Jesus, on the other hand, could see past the rough and ready exterior to the leadership gift that was present. I believe that the leaders that we long for are already present in our churches; our challenge is to identify and develop them.

Perhaps the longing that many church leaders have is for an already established leader to join them, with an impeccable character, a proven track record and gifts that complement what is already present, but in reality this rarely happens. The majority of leaders at Christ Church Manchester are people that I have raised up and developed from within, and this should be a major priority for all church leaders. In my experience, three of the most overlooked groups for leadership are young people, poor people and those that are spiritually immature.

Investing in young leaders is crucial if we are to see churches thriving. As Bob Roberts reflects on explosions of church growth around the world, he says, 'Jesus movements surge from the young.'[36] I have noticed how easy it can be for churches to grow very old in their outlook, and this is something that can happen without anybody realising. Churches that were born out of risk and adventure can become established and move away from those big risky decisions that brought them to life in the first place. People who were radical young pioneers soon settle down to raise kids and get immersed in the (important) business of earning a living and building a career, but at the same time the dynamic spark in the church can simmer down unless fresh young leadership is given the space to emerge.

At CCM, we are ministering in the heart of Manchester, a city that has a great cultural heritage and three thriving universities, and is very youthful in outlook and attractive to young creative people. We have been very deliberate about reaching, engaging and discipling generation after generation of young people. I have found that many of the millennials that we are working with are keen to learn, open to mentorship and hungry for an opportunity to make a difference. I have also found that the mentoring isn't all one-way, and that I have much to learn from these young leaders that I am working with as they keep creating the relevant space for their peers to engage and join in.

It has often been said that the millennial generation has an activist outlook, and a desire to change the world. As a church with a Have a Go Culture, we want to give as much opportunity as possible for this. We often say to the students who come to one of the universities in Manchester or Salford, 'Be a student; plant a church'. We aren't joking; in all of our sites we have young leaders with significant practical leadership responsibilities as they develop their leadership gift.

The second group of people often overlooked for leadership comprises those from poorer backgrounds. People from such backgrounds often don't look like the typical 'Christian leader' stereotype and so can get passed over. In truth, there can be some work to do (as there is with any leader) in helping them untangle which parts of their background are helpful to their leadership and which aren't. In the early stages of developing leaders from challenging backgrounds it can look a bit messy. They are less likely to attend a 'leadership development class' than believers from a more affluent background (although I am not convinced that such a class on its own is the best approach to leadership development for anyone), and a more flexible and organic approach is needed, sharing life and ministry together and discussing the lessons as you go. Just like Jesus did.

The third group of potential leaders is those that have not yet attained to a high standard of spiritual maturity. The most common model I see, in relation to deciding who can lead, is one that starts by considering people whose personal walk with God seems to be in good order and who have demonstrated their commitment to the church through regular attendance and faithful service in other roles. I can understand the rationale behind this, and there is an appropriate biblical caution when appointing people to certain positions, such as eldership, but in general we are way too cautious in who we will entrust responsibility to in the church, and this contributes to our perception of a 'lack of leaders'.

For me, the best way to learn about how to develop leaders is to look at how Jesus himself did it. The people that Jesus called to himself didn't have a particular track record of spiritual leadership, and they still had lots of character issues that needed addressing. Clearly there were two goals that Jesus had for the disciples: they needed to grow in character, and they needed to be trained to take responsibility. What is interesting to me is that Jesus approached these two goals simultaneously. Whereas we might wait until a certain level of progress had been attained in personal spiritual formation, Jesus was ready to entrust them with responsibility straight off the bat. I have tried to take a similar approach, and have found that the two things serve each other well. It is through being given responsibility that people take some of their biggest growth steps in their own discipleship journey, and as they grow personally they are strengthened in the area of leadership they have been given.

It is true that working with leaders who are younger, or from poorer backgrounds or who are less spiritually mature can be risky, and there have been moments when I have needed to come alongside those leaders and help steer them through tricky situations. And yet even this has proven to be tremendously formative, and those leaders have emerged much stronger for it. By trusting people to come into the leadership journey with me, I have built a team of loyal, capable, and dynamic leaders who together have the energy and capacity to continue planting and growing CCM in our city and beyond, to a much greater degree than I would have been able to do on my own.

Leading in a multisite church can be hard. Developing others can be messy, and entrusting things to them can feel like a risk. But the needs are great and the rewards are high, and I am more convinced than ever that, as we lead well, we create an environment where change can be embraced, where a healthy pace is set, where new leaders emerge and thrive, and where the rule and reign of God moves forward. For me, that makes it all worth it!

Chapter Fourteen: Discipleship

When somebody walks into Christ Church Manchester for the first time, there are certain things that I want for them. In the short term, I want them to have an enjoyable experience and feel like the church is a place they could call home. Longer term, I want to see growth and change in their lives. I want them to know Jesus, be part of his kingdom and enjoy his presence. I want them to thrive in their home life and excel in their career. I want them to make deep and lasting friendships. I want them to fulfil their potential, use their abilities and find the part that God is calling them to play in his mission on the earth. This chapter is all about how we do this.

If I am honest, I wasn't quite sure what the right title for this chapter was. In one sense, 'discipleship' is the obvious and biblical word to describe what I am talking about, but I have found that this word can often be hijacked and filled with whatever meaning somebody wants to give to it: from dependency-forming relationships to academic-style Bible study programmes. I wondered if another word or phrase like 'spiritual formation' may serve better but this seems to me quite a one-dimensional term, where the Bible paints a much more holistic picture of what following Jesus involves. In the end I decided to stick with the term 'discipleship'.

In different parts of the Bible, emphasis is given to different aspects of disciple making. It is important to understand a person's personality and temperament in order to find the most effective way of helping them grow. As well, it is important to understand the strengths and the weaknesses of any given approach, and to try to integrate the advantages of each of the different emphases.

Highly relational people are often drawn to Paul's relationship with Timothy, where he calls him a 'true son in the faith'. Building discipleship relationships with this emphasis and terminology can help to cement the family culture that should characterise the relationships in a healthy church. On the other hand, when this kind of terminology is overly used to the neglect of other images, it may build an expectation that can unhealthily lock people into a single individual for a discipleship relationship rather than the church as a whole. In some cultures, the very imagery may imply that the 'father' will also take responsibility for supplying the physical needs of the person and of their extended family.

Paul's exhortation to Timothy to entrust all that he learnt from him to reliable people (2 Tim. 2:2) can motivate organised and systems-orientated people to produce amazing study programmes which really serve to equip people with knowledge and clarity of biblical thinking. Yet in isolation from personal interaction and challenge, these can fall short of teaching people to obey. Head knowledge is good, but on its own it is not enough.

Serving is a significant aspect of being a disciple, and Paul says that the risen Christ has given gifts to equip the church for works of service. However, in so many cases, serving can become primarily about filling rotas, where getting the task done is the be all and end all. Investing in people as they serve by giving the appropriate feedback, encouragement, care and training moves serving beyond merely fulfilling a need into an opportunity to grow and develop.

When Jesus called his first disciples, Simon and Andrew, to himself, he said to them, 'Follow me, and I will make you become fishers of men' (Mark 1:17). This is a holistic call to a new life of adventure and one that we should not hesitate to encourage the people in our churches to share in. Adapting a framework that I heard from my friend, Bryn Hughes, I believe that there are three key elements to growing as a disciple: *proximity, learning* and *opportunity*, as shown in the diagram.

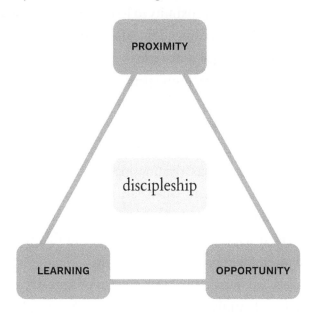

Proximity

The first key element of discipleship is proximity. As Jesus called those first disciples, he started with an invitation to follow him. This would not be a course, a programme or a task but three years on the road together sharing in ministry, life and community with Jesus and with each other. This call is made even clearer, a couple of chapters later in Mark, when Jesus came down from the mountain and appointed them apostles: 'And he appointed twelve (whom he also named apostles) so that *they might be with him* and he might send them out to preach' (Mark 3:14, emphasis added).

Put simply, discipleship at a distance doesn't work. While there can be a place for formal theological education, this cannot be at the expense of relationships of proximity in the local church. It is within a community on mission together that discipleship is worked out, and this means shared lives and proximity. Of course, this begins with proximity to Jesus himself, as discussed in chapter 12, and I would contend that this is the most fundamental component of growing as a disciple.

Having selected twelve, Jesus spent the next few years up close and personal with them. They got to witness miracles: water turned into wine, blind eyes opened, a dead girl raised to life. They got special extra teaching unpacking the parables. They got to witness first-hand Jesus' relationship with his Father. Some of them even got to be there when Jesus was transfigured. Many heard about these events second-hand or observed them at a distance. The disciples were actually there, and that was because Jesus had given them proximity to himself.

As leaders, we must follow this pattern of ministry that Jesus established and minister in proximity to the people that we are serving. Opening our lives in this way requires sacrifice on behalf of leaders. It can feel much more comfortable when we see discipleship as something that happens with somebody for an hour on a Wednesday morning, but truly making disciples means, in the words of Paul, that 'we were ready to share with you not only the gospel of God but also our own selves' (1 Thess. 2:8). This means sharing your table and welcoming people into your home.

It means including people in the mundane things of life, spending unhurried time with no agenda and building friendships. I am often invited to travel as part of my ministry, and where possible I look to invite one or two others along with me. It's a great chance for them to be exposed to another dimension of ministry, and it is amazing how much discipleship can happen over five hours each way on the motorway!

Of course, it should be said that not everybody in your church will have the same level of proximity to you. Jesus chose seventy-two, he chose twelve, and he chose three. Each group had greater access than the previous one. You only have a certain amount of time and capacity, so there is a skill in choosing wisely whom you invest this level of proximity into. However, everybody should have proximity to some leaders in the church. For us this is often site leaders, but could also be community group leaders or other mature believers in their site.

To grow as a disciple we also need to be living our lives in proximity with other believers. Jesus hadn't just called each of the disciples into a personal relationship with himself but also into community with each other. The New Testament contains thirty-eight verses that instruct us to do things to 'one another' (for example, 'love one another', 'teach and admonish one another', 'encourage one another'). It is clear that to grow into maturity in the faith we need one another, and each has a part to play. The Sunday gatherings and community groups do play a part, but it is so much more than this; in each of our sites we are trying to build communities characterised by deep friendships and shared lives (I think that aiming for congregations of around fifty to seventy people definitely makes this easier).

As we live our lives in this way, challenges for growth can be brought to light that would remain hidden when purely book-learning. One example of this was when the disciples of Jesus argued over who could sit on his right and his left in the kingdom. Being in community brought to light their pride and their ambition, and also provided a context in which the issues could be highlighted and worked through. I believe this is part of what it means in Proverbs when it talks about believers sharpening one another as 'iron sharpens iron' (Prov. 27:17).

Learning

The second significant aspect of growing as a disciple is learning new things. The disciples probably heard Jesus teaching most days (and often they would have heard key messages reinforced many times in village after village). When Jesus taught difficult things, they had time and space to process and ask questions. When they struggled with spiritual disciplines like prayer, they could ask Jesus and he showed them how it is done. By the end of three years with Jesus, the disciples had grown in knowledge to such an extent that when they proclaimed the gospel with boldness and clarity the Jerusalem authorities were astonished that uneducated common men could speak in such a way. The only conclusion to draw was that they had been with Jesus.

Theological education does play a part in helping people grow in faith. The more we understand about who God is and what he has done, the more fuel we have for a life of worship and devotion. Of course, there are examples of people who know a lot without living it out, but I would contest that the problem here isn't the knowledge itself but rather the lack of love for Christ!

I have often been frustrated with how good quality theological training can be inaccessible to those who need it most owing to high demands on time, long distances and high costs. I wanted to do something about it, so we set up the CCM School of Theology. On one Saturday morning each month, we invite in a great quality theology speaker, who spends the morning teaching on both Biblical Theology (we are working through the whole of the Bible over two years) and Systematic Theology. We have made this free and available to our whole church, and have been pleasantly surprised at the number (around seventy) and range of people attending. We are now working on similar schools of leadership, preaching and creativity. In addition, we have a fresh sermon at every Sunday meeting, meaning that there are currently six new sermons preached each week, and these are all available online. There are lots of people who stretch themselves by listening to teaching from other sites as well as their own, and I know of some people who love to binge listen to them all!

Along with these front-led learning opportunities, there is also a place for personal input. Jesus knew his disciples well from spending time in proximity with them, as discussed. This meant that he was able to help them personalise what they were learning, encourage them when they did well and call them out when he needed to.

If we want to see the people around us grow then we need to be willing to challenge them. It takes courage to raise uncomfortable issues with people and yet there will be times where this is exactly what we need to do. It also takes skill and compassion to choose your moment well for such conversations, to take time to understand where the person is coming from, to maintain a tone of love and to help them see a constructive path forward.

A word of caution. In my experience, the times where this kind of 'difficult conversation' is needed are less frequent than many people think. If we have the idea that 'discipling' someone basically boils down to telling them off for all the things we think they are doing wrong, then this will create a toxic culture in the church. Much more often it looks like offering encouragement, providing friendly advice, patiently listening and asking provocative questions, and this is the kind of personal input that we should be providing to those around us on a regular basis.

Opportunity

The third component of growing as a disciple is having the opportunity to make a difference. By trade, Simon and Andrew had been fishermen, but now Jesus was promising to make these disciples into 'fishers of men'. They were being given the opportunity to make a difference in people's lives and help build God's kingdom in the world.

As the story unfolds over the next three years, we see the disciples heavily involved in the ministry. They were not merely sitting back and watching as Jesus did all the work. In fact, we read that they were responsible for baptising people (John 4:2), casting out evil spirits (Luke 10:17), and breaking open new ground for Christ's ministry and preaching the gospel of the kingdom (Mark 6:7-13). Following the death and resurrection of Jesus, they had even more responsibility as they were charged with the advance of the gospel to the ends of the earth. Giving people challenging opportunities is not something that should wait until they have made a certain level of progress in their character development. Rather, it is through being given the right opportunities and having a go at making a difference that the progress we long for occurs.

One of the best recent books that picks up on this idea is *Turn the Ship Around!* by David Marquet, a nuclear submarine commander in the US navy.[37] In the book, Marquet tells the story of his time in command of USS *Santa Fe*, a ship that was not doing well when he took over: morale was poor, performance reviews were frequently negative and the retention rate of crew members was very low. Two years later, Marquet had a ship full of happy and empowered crew members who wanted to be there. The rate of officer retention had increased from 0% to 100% and retention of enlisted men had increased twelve-fold. Performance was now being judged, even by the strict standards of the nuclear navy, as excellent. Marquet had truly turned the ship around.

The factor that Marquet felt was most significant in this transformation was a change of leadership style from what he described as 'leader-follower', where the leader sees their role as managing those under them for the successful achievement of shared goals, to a 'leader-leader' model, where they delegate decisionmaking as far down the organisation as possible and trust the judgment and capability of the people working for them. For Marquet this meant giving a level of authority to his officers and chiefs that was unprecedented in the navy, and using the privilege of his own role to make sure they were equipped, able and confident not only to follow orders but to use their skills and creativity to fulfil their mission.

This approach to leadership is simple, biblical and rare. It is rather similar to the advice that Jethro gave to Moses to delegate his judicial responsibilities. As well, it models the approach that Jesus took with his disciples, training and empowering them but also giving them the authority and responsibility for going out two-by-two to the towns and villages of Israel, and then to the ends of the earth.

At CCM we are all about giving people opportunities to do things that will challenge and stretch them. In chapter 6 I outlined our Have a Go Culture. This culture is an important aspect of the way we help people to grow as disciples. Preaching, planting, worship leading and running communities are all things that we want to get as many people as possible involved with, and these people are often young and would perhaps be overlooked by others. The film *Moneyball* (Columbia Pictures, 2011) tells the story of the American baseball coach, Billy Beane. He took a new approach to recruiting his team that was able to unearth the talents and virtues of many who had been overlooked because they didn't fit the conventional mould that others were looking for. I believe our 'have a go' approach to new opportunities allows us to unearth some gems that might otherwise be overlooked.

I am convinced that the multiplanting model particularly helps us at this point. We are creating communities of a small enough size that there is plenty of grace for somebody stepping out and trying something new. There are lots of opportunities to be involved as people are constantly being sent into the next thing. It avoids the leadership roles bottle-necking with a few people. And there is still the resourcing and support of a large church to equip people to reach a standard as they step out into their new opportunities and become all that they can be. A couple of our students took this to heart last year as they pioneered a small group in central Manchester, which has developed into our City Centre site. Having been encouraged by the phrase, 'be a student, plant a church' it is no surprise to us that as students like this move on to different cities and nations they are ahead of their peers in terms of experience, and are often an obvious choice when their new church is looking for pioneers and leaders for new initiatives.

Discipleship is a word that seems to have as many meanings as there are people who use it. For us, it's pretty simple. We want people to grow in closeness to Jesus and to each other, to be transformed into his likeness and to have challenging opportunities to make a difference. I believe that, as this happens, the world will be changed.

Chapter Fifteen:
Creatives

Very early on in the story of Christ Church Manchester, I realised how important it was that we had creative people right at the heart of who we are. Why? Because creative people are game-changers. They see the world in a very different way to the rest of us. I have friends who can stare at a blank piece of paper and see the beginnings of a beautiful work of art, or who can hear a simple chord progression and turn it into a soul-enriching piece of music, or who can look at a problem that has got us all stumped and come up with a solution that takes us off guard by its simplicity and ingenuity. And the frustrating part is that when we ask them how they came up with the genius idea, they give us a blank look. It was just obvious to them.

Inspiration can be so hard to pin down and explain, but the church needs inspiration. It needs creative people who are given space and freedom by leaders to run with their ideas, and who are able to be central to the decision-making process. Craig Groeschel often says, 'If you want to reach people that nobody else is reaching, you will need to do things that nobody else is doing'.[38] Well, I wanted to reach people who nobody else was reaching, and if I was going to do things that nobody else was doing, then I would need some creative people around me to see what those things should be. So I made sure we had such people right at the heart of the church.

What a church looks, sounds, and feels like (both online and offline) has become very important – and it should be noted how much space in the Bible is devoted to various artistic and aesthetic details. You need to be able to articulate your values, your cultures and your strategies in engaging and compelling ways. Creative people can help you with this. In every church that I have planted, the addition of a creative person completely changes what the church can achieve. The church becomes way more fruitful when gifted people are provided with an environment where their gifts can flourish.

Working with creative people is exhilarating and challenging in equal measure. Sometimes creatives can be hard to understand, tricky to motivate, resistant to instruction, or simply difficult to find! You never know what you will get, and much of the time even the creative people themselves have no idea what they are going to come up with. This is certainly not a process that you can micromanage, and you will probably end up in some places you may not have been expecting, but this is all part of the fun!

Musicians, designers, writers and poets are essential to the life of a church, and this needs to be a priority from day one. If you want to reach people who are creative and talented, you need to create a community in which they believe they will be taken seriously and given freedom. Of course, this is much easier said than done. I think back to the time that Christ Church Manchester was a new church plant in Hyde. There were just fourteen of us meeting in a home in an unfashionable area of the city. Young creative people were hardly flocking to join us! However, I knew that if we wanted to pioneer a movement to reach the city, we would need creative ideas. Ten years on we now have crowds of creative people in our ranks, with six worship bands deployed each Sunday, a song writing academy, worship albums with home-made songs, community choirs, writers, photographers, videographers and designers, and mission teams sent out full of people with creative energy.

Getting to this point has been a journey full of laughter, frustration, great nights of worship, ear-splitting nights of noise, money spent, setbacks and challenges, and imaginative and daring moves forward. As with most things in the kingdom of God, prayer and intentionality proved to be the key ingredients in getting something going.

Building with Creatives

The question that I am most frequently asked about building church with creatives is simply, 'Where do I start?' More often than not, creative people want to be in a place that already has a creative vibe where they can see other people like themselves given opportunities to use their skills and do interesting things. This can pose a bit of a catch-22 dilemma for a new planter or a church looking to become more creative. To develop a creative atmosphere you need to attract some creative people. To attract some creative people you need a creative atmosphere. What do you do when you have neither? Perhaps it would help if I shared a bit of our story around this point.

When there were just thirty of us in Hyde, we decided that we were going to start a school of worship and position ourselves as an influential church for the creative arts. I realise that this seems about as realistic as a kid with a wheelbarrow calling themselves a racing driver, but you never know until you have a go! One of the things that is wrapped up in living by faith is daring to dream things that are impossible, and then doing whatever small practical things you can to start moving in that direction. Once we had decided to set up the School of Worship, we started making a lot of noise about what we wanted to do and we prayed hard about it. Out of the blue I got an email from a very talented musician and worship leader asking me if I could suggest a church that he could join in order to learn how to church plant. Bingo! I love emails like that, and my answer is always the same: 'Come to Manchester!'

With this new worship leader taking a lead role, our School of Worship began to take shape. Over the next few years, we ran a number of conferences, gathered crowds of musicians and leaders from across the north, blessed a whole bunch of people, increased our faith for what was possible, and put ourselves on the map as a great place for creative people to be.

A year or so after I got the call from that worship leader, another couple joined us who were looking to build an Eden team with The Message Trust based in Gorton. They were both talented musicians and not long after their arrival doors started opening to pioneer various community activities. One of my personal highlights of this time was a community carol service that was led by local kids and teenagers in a room packed with parents and other members of the community cheering them on.

Without creative people being given the freedom to try ridiculous ideas, none of these would have happened! It hasn't been without financial cost, and they needed the hard work of many volunteers and a tiny staff team. Some of what we tried didn't quite materialise as we hoped, and some of the people who joined us in those early developmental days became disillusioned when we couldn't fulfil everything that we had set our hearts on, and ended up moving on. Hindsight is a wonderful thing, and given my time again there are things that I would have done slightly differently, but I have found that making progress and breaking new ground is often a messy process and most of the lessons that we learn happen on the way.

Our journey accelerated when we pioneered our second site into Manchester's student community. As this site grew, it attracted a new crowd of creative young people into a fun and experimental Sunday evening service. A very different vibe was beginning to form as a disparate group of musicians found one another, and the volume levels kept rising. Despite being the oldest person in the room by a considerable margin (and tone deaf!) I could just about manage to sing along; but they didn't always make it easy for me, throwing in double drum kits, dance music and the occasional punk rock cover of 'Shine, Jesus, Shine'! This congregation was brimming with life, and there was an incredible optimism, peppered with any number of personal dramas that seemed to make simple life choices considerably more complicated than they needed to be.

Many of these creative young people have now become pillars of Christ Church Manchester. We loved them enough to trust them to have a go. We trusted them to create a bit of chaos and to stretch our understanding of what was possible for the kingdom of God! We have been richly rewarded for that trust.

We only got to this place by making bold, intentional steps. We started as a small plant in an unfashionable part of Manchester that was not attractive at all to creative people. Yet through a few deliberate decisions and a lot of prayer we have been able to build a church that is a great place for creative people to hang out.

Embrace the Chaos

The first and most important key ingredient for making creative people feel at home in a church is simple. Love them. We know that we wouldn't be able to create the dynamic, beautiful church that we dream of without them, but this really is a secondary concern. As with anybody else who walks through our doors, we love them much more for who they are than for what they can do.

Needing people and loving them are very different things. I have seen many churches and ministries talk publicly about the value of creative people, where in reality they are thought of as a means to an end rather than as people who need to be cherished, challenged, appreciated, developed and given as much investment as any other leader in the church.

When this foundation of love is in place, this gives space for creative people to try things that might not work, in a supportive and pressure-free environment. In chapter 5 I described CCM's Second Chance Culture. With our young, creative crowd this quickly became a 'seventy-seventh chance culture', but treating people with this grace upon grace is a non-negotiable for us, because it was for Jesus. Forgive me a little rant, but I find it so frustrating when I hear churches talk about the high value they place on the doctrine of grace and yet treat people in an ungracious way. Unfortunately, this can often be what creatives experience in church life, as they struggle to conform to subjective rules and jump through arbitrary hoops in order to use their creative gifts in the church.

The very nature of creativity means that you experiment with things that may work a treat or may fall flat on their face. This is something that you should encourage and learn from. One Sunday evening two of our creative guys led worship from a laptop. They had spent hours coming up with innovative versions of six worship songs and programing them into the sound software, and they had practised very hard. Unfortunately, it didn't work at all, and rather than engaging in the worship, most of the congregation were looking at them blankly with no idea what to do. It was a tough evening, to say the least. However, that wasn't the end of the journey and we gave them the freedom to have another go (as well as lots of feedback). Next time they added a few instruments to the laptop, and that made all the difference. We had a fantastic time together enjoying the presence of God!

Make Winning Easy

In my experience, one of the best qualities that makes a church feel like a fun place to be for creative people is that they are loved and put in a position where they can win often. One of the biggest obstacles towards this, as discussed in chapter 10, is an obsession with excellence. Let's be honest, excellence is not easy to achieve. There are very few people who can produce excellence on their first attempt (and not many who can on their twentieth attempt either). All that a focus on excellence will do is restrict opportunities in the church to all but a tiny group of highly gifted people and cramp out any room for people to grow, develop their craft, practise in the public arena, try new ideas and so grow to a higher standard with their gift.

Having said that, we do still aim high. Everything we do at CCM has both the low bar and the high bar. Getting onto the worship team, the preaching team, the leadership team or the welcome team is easy. The bar is low. Once somebody is on the team, we will help them to develop and reach the high bar.

Making sure that the Think the Best Culture works in practice is very important in ensuring that creatives feel like they are winning. Creating something for public consumption is a brave and vulnerable thing to do, and so it is not surprising that creative people can be self-conscious and worry about how other people perceive them. Creatives quickly pick up on undercurrents of gossip, and will usually sense if you are saying one thing to their face and another behind their back. Our public encouragement needs to be coupled with private praise, both to the person themselves and to others. Our support of them must be both wholehearted and absolute.

One question that we have often been asked is how long a musician needs to have been in the church before they are invited to join the band. For us, it is an easy one to answer; we want them involved as soon as possible. If somebody is playing drums on their second week at the church then this is a very exciting thing for us! Often musicians are amazed to be given opportunities to be involved so soon, but there are good reasons for doing so. Giving creatives the opportunity to be with others like themselves is a very attractive thing, trusting people early in the relationship reinforces the Think the Best Culture that we often talk about, and of course, with multiple meetings across the city every Sunday, we are always looking for more musicians!

Helping people to develop always comes in the context of opportunity. People don't grow in a vacuum; they need to be stretched to the point where they fall back on God in faith and humility. In their excellent book, *Exponential,* Dave Ferguson and Jon Ferguson discuss the importance of a leadership track for creatives.[39] I believe they are right! Currently at CCM we are financing a music producer to facilitate song writing within the church. The aim is to bring some confidence to our song writers, to release some worship music that we enjoy and to let our creatives be creative! It is important to us that our musicians and creatives feel that we believe in them, value them and want them to succeed. This involves much more than using them to fill spaces in the band to make Sundays happen. We want to invest in them as people and help them to be generous with the creative gifts that God has given them to benefit the whole of society.

Some of our musicians are currently working with us in one of the poorest areas of our city, where generations of unemployment and deprivation have throttled aspiration. We see music and the arts as one of the ways that we can serve and bring back dignity and hope to the young people caught up in this vicious cycle. When talented people give time and use their talents to create bands and choirs of young people and give them opportunities to perform and receive applause, often for the first time in their life, it is both inspirational and transformational.

Put Creatives at the Centre

If you want to engage creatives well in your church, it is important that your approach reflects the cutting edge of popular culture (and this culture will have subtle differences from one city to the next, and even from one neighbourhood to the next). This is not to say that you should absorb everything in culture uncritically, but you do need to understand it and minister the gospel in a way that is contextualised to it.

The best way to reach a culture is from the inside, so you need people who are younger and understand your culture to be in leadership roles with real decision-making authority. Because culture is constantly evolving, this means that you need to be always looking to refresh your leadership teams with new emerging creative leaders. It is so easy to get stuck in a time warp where leaders who were at the cutting edge of culture a few years ago are now a bit retro. It can often happen without you even noticing! I have found that multiplanting explodes the leadership bottle-neck that many churches experience and creates plenty of space to bring new leaders through.

Allowing culturally aware creative people, especially those who are young, to be at the heart of decisionmaking is crucial to building effective churches, and I would strongly advocate that at the most senior leadership level of your church there must be young and creative people involved. Wherever the big strategy decisions are made, you need creative minds! This works both ways. If we want our churches to imaginatively advance the kingdom of God then we need creatives involved at a senior level. Equally, if we want to disciple creative young people to grow in wisdom and maturity then they need to be in robust conversation with people who are (hopefully) wiser and more mature than they are.

It sounds obvious, but there is no one better to lead a group of creative people than a creative person who has the spiritual gift of leadership (few things stifle creativity more than a person who is not creatively wired trying to oversee a group of creatives).

Recently I asked one of our site leaders what had made him choose a certain person to lead the teams of musicians at their site. He replied, 'When she arranges a meeting, everyone turns up'. What he had noticed was that the gift of a gathering leader was part of her DNA. We need to be as intentional about identifying and developing the gifts of creative leaders as we are with site leaders and preachers.

Sit Back and Enjoy the Fruit

One of the highlights of our work with creatives was watching some of our musicians on a mission week in Dresden, in the east of Germany, connecting brilliantly with locals in open air performances and worship services. One of the worship leaders on the trip had been a singer with us for a long time, and he took it upon himself to learn guitar within a few months, he led worship five times in a week on the mission trip, and then came back to Manchester and led twice on the Sunday. When I asked him if he minded doing it so much, he grinned at me and said, 'I love it'. This worship leader is producing fruit all over the place.

In one of our sites in a poorer part of Manchester, a lady joined us a few years ago who, in addition to her church involvement, regularly gigs in bands and loves to create music. The leaders at the site worked really hard to engage her and get her involved. She now leads the worship team at this site, helps bring through other worship leaders, is involved in our efforts to produce our own songs, and runs a gospel choir for local teenagers. Not only that, but she's our friend! We trust each other, and she's an integral member of the CCM community.

These are just a couple of examples of how building with creative people at the core has paid dividends for us – there are many more. Seeing creative people who have a passion for world mission, for uplifting poor people and for lifting up the name of Jesus is an amazing thing, and I praise God for the creative people we have in our church who are empowered to use their gifts to see lives and cities transformed.

Chapter Sixteen: Sundays

When we talk about our multiplanting approach, we like to think of it as the best of both worlds. It is a way of building church that attempts to harness the strengths of both larger and smaller churches. Practically speaking, this means that we will aim to have between fifty and seventy people in the room for each of our meetings on a Sunday, which is not far off the average size of a church in the UK.

We believe that our numbers are our strength when it comes to our Sunday meetings. When the number of people in the room is just a few dozen, it facilitates true community. People who are part of our sites will know most of the other people in their site, and will have personal friendships with a high proportion of the people. New people are quickly engaged and drawn into the community. It is noticeable when people are missing, and they can easily be followed up and cared for. There are lots of opportunities for people to step out, use their gifts and play their part in seeing God's kingdom advance.

Because the number of people across the church is much larger than this, it allows us to do things that would not be possible if each site was out on its own. We have built systems for developing preachers, meaning that we have a constant flow of people coming through who can teach God's Word to a decent standard. We have also been able to give a lot of thought to how we do our Sunday services well, and we have developed some key principles that translate across all of the sites.

By aiming for the best of both worlds, we are trying to build sites in which people experience the community feel that fifty to seventy people can generate, coupled with preaching and worship that would usually only be found in a much larger gathering. Even though the number of people in the room is much lower, we teach our leaders to project their voice and govern the meeting as though there were 200 people present. By encouraging this kind of mindset, we change the feel of the meetings from something folksy that is full of in-jokes and comments that would alienate outsiders, to something much more thought-through and inclusive.

As I have spoken of before, I tend to approach different areas of church life with both a low bar and a high bar. Our Sunday meetings are no different. The high bar for each of our sites would include a warm welcome, lots of food and good coffee, a full band that can engage the hearts in worship, and a preacher that challenges and inspires. The low bar means that even when we can't quite hit this, we will do the best we can anyway. Some Sundays it is possible and we can come away feeling like Spurgeon had nothing on us. Other weeks, there can be lessons to learn from things that didn't quite go to plan, and I am OK with that, as long as we do learn from those times and are always growing towards that high bar.

Sundays matter to us at Christ Church Manchester, and there are very deliberate philosophies behind the different elements of what we do in our Sunday meetings. I will outline some of these below.

Preaching Matters

A couple of weeks before one of our newest sites launched public meetings on Sundays, they did a 'dry run' service with just a few of the core team present. A friend of one of the team came along, and in total there were eight people in the room. The preacher on that day preached as though it was a normal service with fifty people there, and taught the Scriptures with passion, insight and clarity. After the service, the person who had visited said that he had only come as a one-off to support his friend, but because of what he had heard in the preach he now wanted to join the church and become part of the core team for this new site from day one. This is the power that good preaching can have, and we see preaching as something that is central to who we are and that we want to leverage across all of our sites.

That said, we have decided against using the video model, or even the single travelling preacher that many multisite churches use. Our heart isn't just to expand the reach of gifted preachers but to raise up many men and women who can teach and apply truth to their own congregations. There is always something of a balancing act between letting people have a go and utilising our more experienced preachers to keep the standard high. The one that we strike appears very attractive to new people, particularly millennials, who place a high value on participation and making a difference.

For us, one of the key requirements of the people that we are raising up as preachers is an openness to instruction. As well as our annual Introduction to Preaching course that runs through the basics of the craft, we have regular training evenings that go deeper into different elements of preaching, plus preaching groups where four or five preachers listen to a recent talk from each member of the group and share feedback with one another. A site leader or other experienced preacher also gives detailed feedback on every sermon preached, focussed around the following seven groups of questions (which closely map to the content taught on the Introduction to Preaching course):

Biblical faithfulness. How well did they handle the Bible passage that they were preaching from? Were the message and points clearly found in the text?

We believe that the Bible is the inspired Word of God, and as such it should be both the basis of the message and the source of the points. We don't want preachers to simply use a text to launch off into their own ideas, but rather faithfully proclaim the heart of their text.

Main point. How clear was the big idea or central thrust of the message? Was there one truth that everybody would take away from it?

A preacher's job isn't to cram everything they know into half an hour, but to bring a coherent and challenging message to people. There should be a single, clear purpose that they are trying to achieve in the sermon, and it should be obvious to anybody who has listened what the main point is.

Personal application. How effectively were they able to connect and apply the message to the lives of those listening? Were they able to do this within the first few minutes of the talk?

Preachers are aiming to see lives changed by God's truth, so it is of crucial importance to help people connect the biblical message to their own lives. This shouldn't just be an add-on at the end of a talk, but right from the start the preacher should be making a promise to the listener of some problem that can be solved, dream that can be fulfilled or need that can be met through the biblical content that they are going to share.

Illustrations. How well did they demonstrate the effectiveness of what they were teaching from their own life and other illustrations?

We are looking for our preachers to show that what they are sharing with people works in practice, through examples and illustrations. In particular, we want some indication that they are living out what they are teaching, and some degree of sharing of their life as well as the message, including testimony as to how the message they are sharing has made a difference to them personally. (There is a place for sharing struggles as well as successes, as long as it is clear that there is some degree of genuine growth in that area of struggle!)

Christ-focussed. How effective was the message at pointing people to Jesus?

The whole Bible is testimony to Jesus Christ, and it is only as we point to him that we will see people saved and changed. From whatever passage somebody is preaching, we want to see them taking the congregation to Christ and his gospel, and doing so in a way that is natural to their passage and doesn't feel forced or cheesy. It is important both to preach the passage and to preach Christ.

Delivery. To what extent did the way the message was delivered add to or diminish from its effectiveness?

The words a preacher chooses, their body language, their pace and tone, their verbal skills, and even the type of notes they preach from, can all be used to powerfully engage people with a message or to distract from and undermine what is being taught. We want our preachers to use every aspect of their delivery to make their message as impactful as possible.

Length. What was the length of the sermon? Did they stay within the time slot they were given?

At CCM we give our preachers a thirty-minute slot. This is long enough to go into depth while still being accessible to newcomers. We feel it is important to honour people's time, and it is important that our preachers keep to the time they have been given. Good communicators are able to share the same material in various degrees of detail, and we expect preachers to adapt theirs to the assigned time.

Worship Matters

Through history, corporate singing has been one of the primary ways that God's people have expressed their worship. For us, this is another key element of what we do when we gather on Sundays. We want to use this time to help people to engage with God, and it is important to us that people are able to connect with both the head and the heart.

To help people engage with the head, we make a point of choosing some songs with rich theological content. It is important to sing the gospel, and that our praise truly reflects who God is and what he has done. Both in the songs that we write ourselves, and the songs written by others, we take great care over the theology. When songs contain ideas that are questionable or open to misinterpretation we will just find some other songs to use instead – there are plenty to choose from! Another element of engaging the head in worship concerns where we place the preach within the service. We do this early, with only a couple of songs before it and a lengthier worship time afterwards, meaning that the praise and worship can come from a place of response to the biblical truth that has been preached.

It is also very important to engage people's hearts. As well as the 'revelation' based songs, we want to create space for 'response' songs, where people can express simple love and devotion to God. We also allow space between songs for people to pray out their own prayers, share encouragements, read scriptures and prophesy. Ultimately, it is the Holy Spirit who leads the gathered body of believers in our worship, and he does so through the different contributions that he gives each one to bring (as outlined in 1 Cor. 14:26-32). I tend to encourage people to bring their contribution from where they are sitting rather than coming to the front, as this encourages the feeling of being a body, and works well logistically with the size of our meetings. I also don't 'vet' the contributions before they are brought, as I want people to be clear that it is the Holy Spirit who is leading the worship time, not the musicians or the elders. Of course, this does mean that there are times when a contribution may need to be redirected or even corrected, but I have found these times to be rare.

Often in churches with smaller Sunday gatherings, there can be a tendency to downplay the worship time because there are only a few musicians in the church. In all our sites we make a big effort to get to a full band as early and often as we can. This can sometimes prove tricky in the early days of a new site, but we have noticed that the presence of a good band tends to be attractive to other musicians. As Jesus said in a different context, 'to he who has, more will be given' (Matt. 13:12). Even on the weeks where we are led by a single musician on a Sunday, we work with them to make sure that we keep a decent tempo, and that the worship 'fills the room' as we look to praise God without timidity.

Communion Matters

We take communion every week in our services, and I would argue that it is the most important thing that we do together, drawing our attention to the cross – the centre of the faith. Because communion is such a big deal for us, we build our services with it right at the centre. It either follows straight after the preach, or one song into the longer worship time, and it gives the service a Christ-centred focus.

Our understanding of what communion is comes from 1 Corinthians 10 and 11, and can be summarised by three words. The first is *remembrance* (1 Cor. 11:24). As we break bread we remember and reflect on Jesus' sacrifice for us. Second, communion is *participation* in the body of Christ (1 Cor. 10:16). Though the bread and wine are not the physical body and blood of Jesus, there is a sense in which we are participating in his body and blood. Communion is a means by which God's grace is made manifest and his presence is enjoyed. Third, as we take communion we *proclaim* the Lord's death until he comes (1 Cor. 11:26). As we lead this time, we are presenting the gospel, something that is beneficial to both believers and non-believers in the room.

Across the sites, there is some bandwidth for how we take communion, and this depends on (amongst other things) the constraints of the room that we are meeting in. In some of the sites we pass around the bread, ask people to take a piece, then pass the wine and invite people to dip the bread in the wine. In other sites we have a table that people can make their way to during the worship time and take communion there. Before people take communion we try to give a good explanation of what it is, and then invite them to participate. As well, we work hard to create a very easy way for people to opt out without feeling self-conscious. We also try to the best of our ability to be as true to the biblical symbolism as we possibly can. There have been moments where newer sites have wanted to 'make do' with Vimto squash, but I have insisted that all of our site leaders use good quality bread and either wine or, at the very least, a good red grape juice. (Providing a non-alcoholic option is very important for people for whom alcohol would be problematic; I believe this is a contemporary application of the instruction to 'discern the body' in 1 Corinthians 11:29).

The Offering Matters

Our approach to finance is discussed in detail in the next chapter, so I won't labour the point here, but I will just say that we take an offering in all of our Sunday meetings and we see this as a great opportunity to teach into this area of discipleship. Before we pass the offering bags, we spend a minute or two sharing a thought from the Bible to set some context for what is happening, and sometimes share a little on what the money will be used for. It only takes a moment or two, but it's such a great opportunity to lead people with faith into generosity and great adventures.

Welcome Matters

In a smaller church gathering, being on your own can be even more isolating than attending a large congregation where you can be lost in a crowd. We have found that having a good and sensitive welcome team, who are easy to spot with badges or T-shirts, is very helpful and not at all over the top.

Sensitivity is key, and there is a balance to strike as you greet newcomers. Of course it is exciting when first-time visitors arrive, and you want to follow up with them and invite them into community, but you want to do so in a way that is neither so pushy that they feel pressured, nor so deferential that they feel excluded. What this looks like can vary greatly for different people. In our experience, undergraduate students and postgraduates are often keen to meet up soon after for a drink, and so we are very intentional on the Sunday about exchanging contact details and meeting up with them the following week. Other people who have growing families and busy jobs may need a little bit longer to find a time that works. We shouldn't be put off by this but work hard to find a time that suits them.

It is important to look out for people who slip into the meetings and sit on their own. When this happens there needs to be somebody near them to introduce themselves and sit with the newcomer. Along with this, having good background music playing before and after the service can make a big difference. The right choice of music can cover any silences without hindering conversations that are happening.

In the early days of one of our site plants, one of the first pieces of advice that I gave to the site leader was to invest in a good coffee machine. By happy coincidence, the site then began its biggest growth surge to date. I still maintain that the coffee had something to do with it! Our hope is that when a new person walks through our door, they are greeted by liberal amounts of good food and great drinks. I think this communicates generosity and places a high value on relationships. People connect and relax when they eat and drink together.

Kids' Work Matters

For many parents who come along to a church, one of the main factors in their decision about whether or not to stick around is what kind of experience their kids have. We have had people at Christ Church Manchester who have told us that the primary reason they joined the church is because their kids had such a good time in our children's work, so we know that this part of our time together on a Sunday is very important indeed.

Kids' work can be a challenge when starting new sites, however. When there are just a handful of adults, there are even fewer kids, and this makes it tempting to ignore the need to do kids' work well. A big effort has been made, as we have started new sites, to have something fun and engaging going on for the children along with the service. Even in the rare situation where the planting team for a site doesn't contain any families with young kids, we make sure that there are people with activities ready to go when such families do show up.

Anchoring Matters

The key role on a Sunday, in my opinion, belongs to the person who is anchoring or leading the meeting. This person has the responsibility for providing direction and keeping momentum all through the service, and this person arguably shapes the experience that people have even more than the preacher does.

One of the top priorities for the anchor in a meeting of our size is making sure visitors feel included and understand what is happening at each point in the service. We want to communicate warmth, but it is important to do so without using in-house language.

Delivering the notices is another part of the role of the anchor. On more than one occasion, I have observed where the person doing the notices doesn't know the basic details about what they are announcing and is corrected by somebody in the congregation. This must be avoided! For me, the notices should be short, sweet and packed full of vision. If the anchor needs written prompts that is fine, but reading details from a phone doesn't look good at all – a piece of paper on a clipboard or lectern is much better.

Sundays matter a lot for us. They are worshipful, community building and mission focussed. We start low, we aim high, and we enjoy the journey.

Chapter Seventeen: Finance

One of the things that has always amazed me at Christ Church Manchester is how much we have been able to do with so little. The first site that we planted was into a part of East Manchester that is one of the most deprived regions in the UK. After this, we planted two congregations by the universities, mainly reaching people who were living off their student loans. Along the way we have reached some working families and graduates, but we are far from a wealthy church, and the highest earners among us would be earning (and giving) a fraction of what the highest earners in many UK churches are.

Two factors, in my view, have converged to allow us to punch above our weight financially. The first is the generosity of our people. This is part of the culture of the church, discussed at length in chapter 8. Our people really do stretch themselves in their giving, and we are thankful for their generosity. The second factor is that we have developed some principles for managing our finance that have helped us make the most of what we have. In this chapter, I want to share some of those principles with you.

Budgeting: Know the Ins and Outs

The first principle that we have developed is to know the ins and outs of our finances. We know the ins (the giving, the Gift Aid, the grants) and we know the outs (the staff pay, the hall hire, the Sunday refreshments, and other numerous odds and ends an active church spends money on). We don't tend to keep to what would conventionally be termed as a 'tight budget' (sticking to a strict financial plan) but we do stay aware of the state of our finances so that we can notice and respond quickly if things are not as we would expect.

Our magnificent treasurer, Jamie Semple (who became a Christian at CCM as a student a few years ago, did a gap year with us and is now a qualified accountant; a prime example of the fruit that the Have a Go Culture can bear), has put together a bespoke financial management system for a multiplanting church that stacks up favourably against even the systems used in much larger churches. Using this system keeps the finances exceedingly well-organised, with both an easy to grasp summary dashboard for site leaders and trustees to access and a much more detailed breakdown of figures including, when necessary, up-to-the-day tracking that we can pore over.

Knowing the ins and outs of our finances allows us to anticipate future growth in giving, and allows us to plan how we can use these resources to further the kingdom and bring to fruition the things that God has put on our heart. We budget annually for the year ahead, providing the site leaders with rough guidelines for what we think an increase in site giving might look like, and what we think they'll need to spend in order to keep things running. We don't correlate the income that a site receives with the money it has available to spend, but we do ultimately hope that all sites will give generously and become net contributors. There is a lot of freedom for site leaders to reallocate money among budget lines, but in general we would expect them to stay within the broad parameters of the budget that has been set (or if not, to make a case in advance why they might need to spend more). Site leaders are sent a monthly summary of the finances and are pretty good at staying on top of things in this regard.

As well as the updates that we send to site leaders, we put together an annual financial report for the congregation. We are aware that there are some people who love this kind of information and will scrutinise it in great detail, while there are others who trust us to get on with it and don't really want the details. We have found that giving out the report in a written format serves both groups well, and that people can engage with it at whatever depth they like. Transparency in our finances is important, so along with the report, we make it clear that we are happy to sit down and discuss whatever follow-up questions people want to ask about our finances.

Budgeting: Full of Faith

One of the challenges of church finance is navigating the tension between fiscal responsibility and faith for kingdom growth. Whilst we don't want to act in an irresponsible manner, I think it is important that we lead out in faith in every area of church life, and this includes our budget.

When we put together our budget each year, we do so with the expectation that we will grow. We assume that more people will join the church, grow as disciples and, as part of this, give financially. As such, we budget as though our income each year will be higher than the year before, and we spend money on new sites and initiatives that will help bring about this growth. It is easy to talk about faith for growth, but for us a part of this has been a willingness to budget in accordance with this faith.

Even with optimistic growth projections, when we have been making our budgets in recent years, we have felt God calling us to pioneer lots of exciting new initiatives and have wanted to respond to these calls; thus we have budgeted with faith that God will provide the resources for these initiatives. Often this has meant that we end up projecting to spend more than we expect to receive. Funnily enough, as we have stepped out in this way we have almost always found that we have either received more or spent less than we expected and the figures have balanced. Budgeting with this kind of faith isn't something that we do lightly, and we do have some money in the church reserves that we could draw on if required. It is also something that we have done with the full support of the treasurer and the trustees, who are great at encouraging the church leaders to step out and lead by faith.

One of the most drastic examples of this was when we wanted to plant our second site into Fallowfield. We had the opportunity to bring Tim Simmonds to Manchester to lead the plant, and so we emptied our bank account to hire him full-time for a year (with no promises of employment beyond the year). This was a big risk, and it is unlikely we will take a risk on this scale again, but it set the trajectory for what the church has become and I don't regret it in the slightest. Even though we had committed all of our savings to hiring Tim, we had grown to such an extent that, at the end of the year, the money was still there in the account. This has been a common experience for us: budgeting to grow, and even then to lose money, but in the end not losing a penny. I can't promise that the same will happen for you if you budget the same way, but I do know that God is a generous provider and that he loves us to step out in faith and see what he will do.

Pioneering: Starting Small, Dreaming Big

I recently heard an interview with Jonas Kjellberg, the entrepreneur and investor who is best known as the co-creator of Skype, the founder of Player.io and the chairman of iCloud.[40] One of the things that Kjellberg talks about is 'innovating in zeros'. The idea is that whilst many innovators will be always looking to add more benefits and features to their products, Kjellberg tries to use his innovative mind to remove the costs that create a barrier for entry. For example, when he created Skype, Kjellberg was able to find a 'zero' by removing the costs of phone infrastructure, and developed a way to channel calls through the internet connection that people were already paying. By finding several such 'zeros' they were able to create something that was high quality but low cost.

This is similar to the approach that we take to pioneering new churches. I have already talked about how we start with a relatively small number of people. This is our first 'zero', and it means that we can keep on planting more sites without causing too much of an issue for the sites they are planted from.

This small number of people also gives us our second 'zero', which is finance. Pastoring a group of fifteen to twenty people doesn't take loads of time, and so we usually start by offering just one day per week of employment to the site leader (we have even planted with volunteer leaders in the past). We also don't need a particularly big venue. We tend to take a 'cheap and cheerful' approach to where we meet in the early stages, and we have found that such venues are in plentiful supply. All things included, we have found that we need to budget about £13,000 for the first year of a church plant, including the cost of the venue and one day per week of staff time.

As the site grows, this cost will obviously increase. There will be a need for a bigger room, more hospitality costs and more staff time (we tend to see a site of around fifty people as needing two days of staff time per week). Once a site has reached fifty people we look to plant out from it again, and the aim is that in time every site becomes a net contributor to the whole.

Staffing: Part-Time and Bivocational

As Christ Church Manchester employs new staff, it is almost always on a part-time basis. I mentioned in the section above that we tend to start new site leaders on one day per week and look to eventually increase this to two days. We have found that employing people part-time has been a very effective way of keeping things lean and multiplying rapidly. At the time of writing we have a staff team of ten, only two of whom are employed by the church on a full-time basis. All of us have at some time worked on a part-time bivocational basis, and most of us still work in that way.

From the perspective of the church, this takes the pressure off our new initiatives to succeed quickly. Paying a full-time salary would commit a sizeable proportion of our budget to a single project, and this cost would probably mean that we had to say no to other things that we would like to do but could no longer afford. By putting so many of our resources in a single place, we would be creating an unhealthy expectation for quick growth, particularly growth in giving capacity. Some of the places that we would like to plant in are difficult communities that will need a slow-burn approach and that may never end up generating loads of money. Our incremental approach to staff time allows this kind of initiative to grow at a natural pace.

When we increase the hours of a staff member, we tend to do so a day at a time to meet a specific need. If we find somebody has more on their plate than their time allows, we will open a conversation about increasing their employed time or giving a day to somebody else to share a bit of the load. Sometimes it takes a little bit of time to catch up with the needs, and grow financially to a place where we can afford the extra time that we require, but it is an important principle for us that the seasons that we ask people to be stretched in this way are brief, and that we honour our workers by paying them their due.

We never promise anybody that their part-time hours will turn into full-time, and many of the team have built lives that work well around part-time hours. Some of our team have young children, and have combined their part-time work for CCM with some days of staying home with the kids while their partners also work part-time for other organisations. We have people who work a couple of days for us alongside a postgraduate course, and others who combine multiple income streams to make a full-time role.

I am not set against employing people full-time in principle, and may do it again in the future, but I usually find that the value that is added by increasing an existing member of staff from three days to four is probably less than the value of bringing on somebody with an entirely different skill set for one day per week. In general, I have found that this part-time and bivocational approach to staffing is something that has worked very well for us.

Giving: A Discipleship Issue

Amongst many church leaders, and particularly church planters, there can be nervousness about bringing up the topic of money, but I see it as a great opportunity to disciple people. It is, after all, a topic that Jesus came back to over and over again in the gospels, and in my experience, people are usually more open to talking about it than we might expect.

I have found it very helpful to talk about money in a holistic way. Often churches can have a reputation for only bringing up the topic when we are asking people to give, but I want people to learn how to thrive financially. The Bible has a lot to say about working hard and earning money, about saving and planning for the future, about spending and enjoying what you have, as well as about giving and generosity. John Wesley once said, 'Earn all you can, give all you can, save all you can'. I want to help my people to have a well-rounded and mature approach to their finances, and help them understand giving as part of a much bigger whole.

We try to do a sermon series at every site of the church that explores different areas of finance at least once every couple of years, sometimes more regularly than that. As we are discipling our people we will often talk about their approach to work and money. Many people just haven't really given it much thought before, and even raising the topic helps them to start to think about changes that they can make.

When it comes to giving, I want people to see that it is a discipleship issue. Following Jesus means laying everything down under his lordship, and it doesn't make sense to say that Jesus is Lord over everything except my wallet! Mature Christian discipleship includes generous giving, to the church and in many other settings. I am trying to raise up a church full of people who are both eager to give regularly to fund the mission of the church, and quick to volunteer to buy a round of drinks when they are out with friends.

Generosity: A Kingdom Culture

God is generous, and as people being remade in his image, we want to reflect that same generosity to others. Generosity is about more than giving cash, it is about behaving towards others as God has behaved to us. It is a key strand of the culture of our church, and in chapter 8 I unpacked what this means and some of the implications of it for church life. Some of the ways in which this culture has impacted our church finances follow.

The Generous Culture has an important effect on the way that we run our finances. Put simply, we give loads away. Every year we have two big special offerings, one of which is entirely given away to poor people (and parts of the other are usually given away too). We also start and fund initiatives like the Broadcast Network that trains and supports church and site planting, a School of Theology and a School of Leadership that we give away free to the wider church. As well, we are constantly looking to invest money into getting the next new plant started.

The other side to the Generous Culture is that it is contagious. It's been notable that as we have sown generously in our spending, we have also reaped generous giving. As I said at the beginning of this chapter, the generous giving of our people is a big factor in enabling us to do as much as we have. I am constantly thankful to God for the generous church that I have the privilege of leading.

Chapter Eighteen:
Communication

One of the most common challenges that I have noticed in multisite churches, and particularly in churches with a model like ours, concerns communication. You have a church made up of lots of different people, based in different sites, with different levels of responsibility and different levels of desire to be in the know. Some people thrive on hearing all about what is happening across the city and beyond. Others are way more energised by what is going on locally to them. The challenge is to ensure that everybody has all the information they need and feels like part of the process, without overloading them with details that are not relevant to them and that they neither need nor want to hear about.

Of course, communicating well is necessary for every church, but the challenge is accentuated when you are multiplanting. There are people in the church who are rarely in the same room as the senior leader on a Sunday. Site leaders have a place on the front line of communicating vision, so their engagement is key. So too does any centralised administrative or operations team that you have, as they have an important role in building systems and managing your digital communication (which is more important than ever).

In the early days of CCM, much of the communication happened quite organically. We were a small church with a single congregation, so I was naturally involved in lots of day-to-day conversations with all the different stakeholders in our church. In these conversations, vision and ideas flowed, and they were supplemented with announcements from the front or text messages, as necessary. At this point communication was pretty easy.

When we started our second site, it met at a different time of day to the first one, so I was usually present at both, as were a few of the other leaders in the church. Again, we muddled through with a mainly organic system of communication. By the time we started site number three, it was becoming apparent that this kind of communication was getting a bit stretched and was no longer fit for purpose. We needed to start building some systems to be much more deliberate about how we would communicate with the church. In hindsight, we probably left it a bit too long getting to this stage. I would say the moment you have more than one site, building in some good communication systems is a must.

Over the years since, these systems have evolved with both the changing needs of the church and the developments of communication methods in our culture (there was a time when you could you send out a mass email and expect the majority of people to read it; today you will be lucky if a third of people do). Because the specific systems are constantly changing, in this chapter I will focus more on the principles behind the systems than the specific methods we are using, and finish with a few tactics that are proving to be effective for us at the moment.

Communication is Your Responsibility

As the senior leader of the church, I know that ensuring that communication is done well is my responsibility. There will always be miscommunications. A few months ago a meeting had been organised and I was hoping for a particular couple to be there, but they were only told about the event a few days before and already had other plans. Whilst there might be an instinct to blame members of my team for not checking with them, or to blame the couple themselves for not looking ahead on the church calendar and noting the event, I know that the mistake here was mine; I wanted them at the meeting but I didn't actually speak to them about it.

In the early days of CCM, taking responsibility for communication meant that I did a lot of the communicating myself. As we have grown, much more is now driven through our operations team. But I still have a role to play in this, and as we move things forward I need to ensure that I am having the right conversations with the right people to ensure that everybody is on board and engaged with where we are going.

Communication is about much more than telling people the time and date of an event. I want people to understand our vision, and to share it, and this doesn't happen just by reading an email or listening to a sermon. In our model, our site leaders have a critical role in helping people to understand what we are about, and so it is imperative that they have fully bought in to what we are doing. A lot of my time is spent in coffee shops with these leaders, chatting about how things are going. These meetings are usually informal and the agenda is either loose or non-existent, but through this kind of regular communication, vision is gradually understood and owned and culture is caught. As trivial as these conversations sound, they are where great communication starts.

When we have a decision to make about a new initiative or a change to something we are currently doing, I make a point of having these conversations in a much more intentional way. I want to understand what people think about an idea before bringing it into a meeting, because this will help me know how to lead the meeting. If I know that everybody is in agreement with an idea then I can lead a faith-filled meeting that is focussed on the practicalities of making it happen, whereas if one or two have reservations then there will need to be a much slower conversation, going through the arguments for and against and seeking to hear and alleviate the concerns and bring those people on board. If I find that most people don't like the idea, then I need to hear that and reconsider what we are planning or at least the way I am putting it across.

In a similar way, once a meeting has happened where it seems like a decision has been made, I try to get on the phone with the people in the room either later that day or the next day and ask them how they are feeling about things. I know that sometimes people will be swept along with the consensus in the room only for questions or doubts to emerge when they have had time to process things. I want to make sure that I am fully hearing what people are thinking and truly bringing them with us in the decision we have made.

At the moment, our Operations Team is headed up by Tom O'Toole, who also leads our site in central Manchester. I love the way Tom leads discussions in our team meetings, and I find that I often ask him to steer us through a particular topic that we need agreement on. Tom usually starts by clearly articulating the issue at hand, perhaps introducing a couple of scriptures, and then asks for some thoughts from the room before building on these to help us reach some shared thoughts.

A good example relates to a staff team meeting we had a few days after the 2017 Manchester bombing. We needed to decide what we would do differently in our upcoming Sunday meetings to appropriately respond to the events a few days before. In introducing the topic, Tom described two possible scenarios – we ignore it completely or we do a full memorial service – and he described these options as 'zero' and 'ten'. He then went around the room asking where on the scale people thought our response should be. Naturally, most people chose somewhere between four and six, which led nicely into a discussion of what things we should do and what we should avoid. Had Tom just steamed in from the start with a list of dos and don'ts, it is doubtful he would have brought people with him anywhere near as well as he did.

Communicate with Vision

One of the best ways to understand what effective communication looks like is to think about what it is like being at the other end of the process. Many of us know what it is like to have an inbox filled with messages from companies telling us about themselves, and we usually dismiss them as meaningless clutter. As hard as it may be for us to believe, much of the communication from our churches is received in just the same way.

A good approach to communication has to be about more than whether you have told people something or not. You might have said it in the notices on a Sunday (a lot of people switch off at this point in the service), sent an email (not everyone will have read it) or posted it on social media (you're at the mercy of the algorithms as to whether people even see it). You need to think about more than simply whether or not you have said it, but whether or not what you are saying has been heard and understood. This is altogether more complicated and means that you need to pay attention to factors like how you say it, who says it, when you say it and what channel of communication you choose to employ. If you want to break through the clutter, it's important to find a way of convincing the people that what you are saying matters. To do this you need to bring vision front and central in everything you communicate.

Simon Sinek highlights this very point in the most viewed TED talk of all time, 'How Great Leaders Inspire Action.'[41] He explains that many companies and organisations (and the same could be said of churches) communicate by telling people what they are doing, and perhaps how they are doing it. Sinek argues that 'People don't buy what you do; they buy why you do it'. His suggestion is that rather than starting with 'What', we start with 'Why'. Cast vision to people for why you do what you do, then follow it with 'How' you intend to accomplish that and only thirdly talk about 'What' precise steps you intend to take.

All communication should be visionary. You should be speaking to people about your values, vision and culture over and over again. We have talked about the dream of starting twenty churches so much that the most frequent question I get asked when I announce a new plant is, 'Where will we plant after that?' This is a good thing. When you have a specific event that you want people to come to, help them to see how it fits into the vision and you are much more likely to inspire them to be there than you would simply by saying what the event is.

Developing Your Voice

Whenever you communicate, you do so with a particular voice. By this, I mean the way you say things, what words you choose, where you place your emphasis and the general tone that you use. Your voice is very important because it reveals a lot about what you value as a church. This may be in line with what you say your values and culture are, or it may serve to undermine them. For example, a church that has a stated value of inclusivity but in its Sunday services makes a lot of in-jokes that go over the heads of visitors has shown that the inclusivity value may not be as strong as they would like to think.

Voice is something that you can control, and it is far better to hone your voice deliberately than for it to develop accidentally without any thought. If you have other people such as site leaders or an operations team that speak on your behalf, make sure you take time to help them catch the voice that you have developed. This is particularly important in a multiplanting church because you won't even be in the room for much of the communication that happens, and when the messages coming out of one site or ministry area carry a very different tone from what you are building, this can confuse people and will actually be very damaging for the cohesion and growth of the church.

What follows are some of the characteristics of the voice we have developed at Christ Church Manchester.

Positive. This is an outworking of our Think the Best Culture. We want to project hope and faith into everything that we do. It is possible to say similar things in very different ways. A few years ago, someone who was new to our communication team wrote a piece about spiritual gifts in worship with the title, 'How to Ruin a Church with Your Gift'. I suggested he changed the emphasis to 'How to Bless a Church with Your Gift' instead because he could still make the same points but do so in a way that is much more congruent with the CCM voice.

Outward-focussed. We want to make a big effort to ensure newcomers or those looking on from the outside don't feel isolated or alienated by our communication. We try not to make in-jokes, and if we refer to things that have happened previously in church life we try to say a few words to give people who don't know about them a bit of context. Similarly, if our communication requires complex language or technical jargon, we do what we can to explain it to people in simple terms.

Smart casual. For a church like ours that has fairly informal services and is frequently trying new things, adopting an overly formal style of communication would seem out of place and would probably alienate people. On the other hand, when the way we communicate is too informal it is tricky to convey the importance of the things that we are trying to get across, and can come across as a bit flippant or irreverent to people from certain cultural backgrounds. We try to keep things 'smart casual' where we can.

Accurate. We want to put our message across in a way that is clear and easy to understand. We have also worked hard to ensure that everybody who is communicating on our behalf is equipped with the correct details for the things they are talking about (site leaders and service anchors are sent weekly briefings from our central operations core, including key information for their own awareness and specific details of notices for Sunday services). When our communication is in written form, it must be both factually accurate and grammatically correct.

How to Communicate

I have found that whenever there is something new going on in the church, I need to communicate it with different people in different ways depending on their level of leadership within the church and also how directly they will be impacted by the decision. There are some people who need to be told in person by myself or another senior leader, whilst others are happy to find out in a much more impersonal way, such as a notice on a Sunday or a link to a post on the church website. There are also some people who need a fairly in-depth explanation of what is happening, why we have reached that decision and how it will work in detail, whilst others would prefer a much briefer summary.

Each group of people corresponds to a different quadrant on the diagram. I find it helpful to take into account each of the quadrants when I need to communicate about a new decision, project or event.

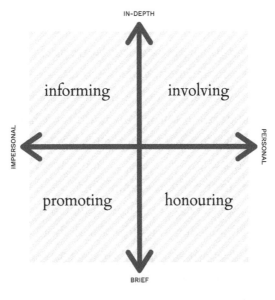

It is important to take each of the quadrants in the correct order, and I always start with the top-right quadrant. These are people whom I want to engage in a personal and detailed way, because I want to *involve* them in the decision. These will often be key leaders, either of the whole church or of a specific site, who are particularly affected by the decision. For example, the idea was recently suggested of changing the name of one of our sites to make it fit better with its local community and make it more consistent with how we have named our other sites. Before we could go anywhere with a decision like this, I wanted to make sure that the leadership team of that site were part of the conversation, so we made sure that we had the conversation with them in person and in detail. By doing this, we made certain that they were in agreement with the decision, and we were actually able to improve the idea as we took on board other linked suggestions that they had.

A mistake that I have seen many leaders make is that once they have involved the key people and made a decision, they then go public with what they have decided. However, before doing this there are other people whom you should talk to about what you have decided. These are people who don't need to be directly involved in the decision but who would find it helpful to know what is happening; briefly mentioning it to them in person would *honour* them in the process. This is the bottom-right quadrant of the diagram. In the recent example, this would be the people who lead our other sites. The name change doesn't affect them very much at all, but they might be asked about it by people in their sites and it sets them up well if they are aware of what is happening, and why, before it is publicly communicated.

Once you have spoken in person to the people who you need to involve or honour, you are now ready to *inform* a larger group by sharing the details of what you are doing; and remember to start with 'why'. There will probably be too many people in this group to personally inform them all, so you will need to utilise more impersonal means, such as an email, a YouTube video, a notice in a Sunday service or church family meeting, a letter, or ideally a combination of several of these things. Keeping an up-to-date central database with email addresses and phone numbers is critical to our communication (making sure to comply with all data protection regulations), and there are good tools that help manage this. With our name change, we went for an email, a video and a mention in the Sunday services to make sure the message got out there to everybody who would want to know. By the end of this process we want everybody to understand what is happening, to know how it affects them and to be able to articulate the rationale behind what we are doing. It is a good idea to also make yourself or others who were involved in the process available for more personal follow-up if people have questions or would like to discuss things further.

Finally, once everyone who needs to know has been informed, you may want to try to get the word out further by *promoting* or advertising what you are doing. People on the outside of your church probably won't want to be bombarded with lots of details, so you are looking for something that is short and attention-grabbing, that is accompanied by a way for people to access more details if they want (for example, you might post an interesting graphic on Facebook, accompanied by a link for more information). By working through these quadrants in the right order, you will help the people in your church to feel empowered and informed as you move forward, and to share in the pioneering journey with you.

Top 10 Communication Tactics (For Now, Anyway)

Most of what I have discussed in this chapter is timeless. This is deliberate, as I want you to understand some principles that will help your church communicate well, wherever the technological and cultural trends shift. To finish, I want to share a few pointers that are not necessarily timeless, but are working for us at the time of writing. You might find these helpful or you might find them hopelessly outdated, depending on when you are reading this.

1. Your website is a front door. Aim it at people outside your church and use it to tell your story.

2. Google search can be your best friend. It takes hard work to rank high for 'church in YOURTOWN' but the reward is worth the effort.

3. Google ads are not good value for money. Facebook ads may be, but you need to choose your target audience for them cleverly.

4. When using social media, video gets more engagement than images. Images get more engagement than just text.

5. It is important to pick your moment for communication, and there are great scheduling tools that can help you with this. Proverbs 27:14 is in the Bible for a reason.

6. Personal social media accounts tend to have more reach than corporate ones. We find that posting on the church accounts and then sharing on personal ones works well.

7. Don't brag about your church/ministry on social media. Retweeting compliments looks bad (replying and/or liking them are much better responses).

8. Each platform has its own 'rules'. If you post identical content on Instagram and Twitter, you're using (at least) one of them wrongly.

9. Group chats are helpful up to a certain number of people (around twelve). Above that, they are just annoying.

10. Arguing on the internet rarely solves anything. Stay classy.

Putting It into Practice

Start with Small Steps

When I returned from the United States in 2006, and began the second phase of my ministry in Manchester, I took leadership of a core group of a new church plant named East Manchester Family Church (later renamed Christ Church Manchester). Over time, I managed to add a few to the original group of fifteen with a heart for reaching that part of the city. Quite quickly the church began to get established in the east, but I knew when I started talking about pioneering and going to the next place that it didn't make sense to everybody. Some hadn't seen this approach to church before and couldn't really imagine it.

I know that if I had tried to do too much too soon, it would have been difficult for people to understand and would have destabilised what we had already built. I was living in the reality that most changes cannot be made all at once, so instead of trying to change everything, I needed to find a small step that would make sense in my context. For me, this involved finding a handful of people who did get it and helping them have a go at doing something in a different part of town. It was such a small number of people that the impact was barely felt on the original congregation, and because it met at a different time of day I was able to be involved with both. This step caused minimal disruption to the East Manchester congregation and the risk factor was low. If it hadn't worked out, then there would have been no harm done. It did, however, and before long had grown into a second congregation of a similar size. By seeing this new congregation emerge, people could witness for themselves what we were trying to do.

The next steps on the way were working out how to be one church that had two congregations. We addressed questions about what things were shared and what things were decided at site level. Because it comprised only two sites this was quite an organic process, and it made sense to people. They could see why we needed to work these things out, and they engaged in the process. When we planted the third congregation there was a little bit more understanding of what was going on amongst the congregation, because they had already seen it working, but in truth this congregation stretched us more than the second one ever did because now we had multiple congregations meeting at the same time. Key leaders couldn't be everywhere and delegated authority became the order of the day.

Each new congregation that we have planted has raised new questions about how we relate together as one church. The challenges change as the scale increases, but each has seemed like an achievable step at the time we have taken it.

In your own context, you probably have things going on that are working well and other areas where you are a bit stuck. Trying to change too much at once is likely to be counter-productive. You need to identify the first small steps that can help you get where you want to go.

Perhaps some of these steps could include the following:

- *Start a new midweek group* in a community where you have a few people and would like to plant in the future, and start praying about how the group can become the core of a new site or church plant.

- *Identify a couple of pioneering leaders* who you can invest in and develop as leaders for a new plant.

- *Hold some prayer meetings* about reaching your whole city or region. Be open to the leading of the Holy Spirit and ready to respond to what he calls you to do.

- *Connect with trans-local ministry* and hear stories of global gospel advance. Invite people to come and help you figure out the next steps for reaching your own context.

Start with Pioneers

At a recent church and site planting conference, the guest speaker was the Australian missiologist Steve Addison, who unpacked a model of growing churches through street evangelism and discipleship. What Steve brought was very challenging and inspiring for many of us when it comes to our own approach to evangelism. It is also something that, if adopted absolutely, could require some serious overhauls to church life and structure. In the question and answer time, somebody picked this up and asked Steve where he would recommend starting for a church that is already going pretty well and for whom a major overhaul would be unhelpfully disruptive.

A lot of the advice that Steve gave echoed the ideas that I have shared in this chapter. He suggested to the leader asking the question that if things are working well, not to do anything to change that but maybe to find a few people who are keen to have a go at the street work and start something small scale on the side. If it began to see fruit and get traction then it could easily grow into something bigger.

My advice for multiplanters would be the same. You don't need to start by disrupting what you are already doing in church, and it is unlikely that the majority of your people will understand what you are trying to achieve until they have seen it in action. But there will be a few people who do buy into it straight away. These are your early adopter pioneers and they are the people to start with.

My suggestion would be to identify three or four of these people (potentially a few more) and get them excited about a vision to reach a region. Together, identify where is the 'next place' (this may be another community in your city, or a neighbouring market town in a rural context) and commit to starting a midweek meeting there. Find a home or a public space in that community and start meeting together, praying, discussing the Bible, and having food and fellowship with one another.

If you can make a little bit of noise about it and create a fun place to be, before long you will add a few more to your numbers. The initial pioneers may not be the people who build long-term (they may well be the ones who go off and start the next thing… and the one after that) but over time a community is formed and a plant can be established. The pioneers are the scaffolding that makes it work long enough for others to understand what it is about and get involved. Finding these people is the crucial first step towards a multiplanting church that reaches a region.

The Power of Pioneering

James Hudson Taylor is one of my heroes of the faith. Taylor went to China in 1853, and unlike many of the other Western missionaries who were there at the time who stuck to the coastal regions, he immediately had a vision for reaching the whole of China. In fact, the historian Ruth Tucker described Hudson Taylor's missionary work in this way: 'Few missionaries in the nineteen centuries since the Apostle Paul has had a wider vision and has carried out a more systematic plan of evangelising a broad geographical area than did James Hudson Taylor.'[42]

Immediately after he arrived in China, Taylor adorned himself with local clothing and wore a pigtail in the Chinese style (this was unique amongst Western missionaries). He headed inland, with a dream of bringing Christianity to every province and village in China.

In order to make this happen, Taylor needed to carry the vision but also recruit and release others into the mission. After some time back in England to recover from an illness, Taylor returned to China in 1866 with sixteen additional missionaries to send to the different provinces. By 1876, this number had increased to fifty-two. In 1884, a further seventy-six were added to this number and, in 1887, another cohort of 102 missionaries joined them.

By pioneering and always looking to the next place, Taylor started a movement of missionaries known as the China Inland Mission that was able to bring the good news of Jesus to every part of China. They rooted the gospel so deeply in Chinese soil that even a century later when Chairman Mao expelled foreign missionaries, he couldn't stop the kingdom growing and less than a million believers multiplying into many millions.

My prayer is to see a similar kind of gospel growth in my region and in yours. This is why I pioneer. This is why I multiplant.

Endnotes

1. https://www.eauk.org/church/research-and-statistics/english-church-census.cfm
2. Malcolm Gladwell, *The Tipping Point* (London: Abacus, 2001), p.177-181
3. Brad House and Gregg Allison, *Multichurch* (Grand Rapids, MI: Zondervan, 2017), p. 48.
4. http://www.thebroadcastnetwork.org/church-planting/gods-promises-vision-church-plant/
5. Attributed to management guru Peter Drucker.
6. NT Wright, *Jesus and the Victory of God*, (London: SPCK, 1996) p. 276.
7. John Maxwell, *Developing the Leader Within You* (London: HarperCollins, 2001) p. 162.
8. Joachim Jeremias, *New Testament Theology* (London: SCM, 1971) p.115-16
9. John C. Maxwell, *Developing the Leaders Around You* (Nashville, TN: Thomas Nelson, 2006) p. 69.
10. https://en.oxforddictionaries.com/definition/cynicism
12. https://open.life.church/resources/2749-making-change
13. http://www.thebroadcastnetwork.org
14. Bob Roberts, *The Multiplying Church* (Grand Rapids, MI: Zondervan, 2008) p. 62.
15. http://www.pewforum.org/2015/04/02/christians/
16. Andy Stanley, *Next Generation Leader* (New York: Multnomah Books, 2003) p. 52.

17. John Kotter, *"Leading Change: Why Transformation Efforts Fail,"* HBS No. 710-455 (Boston: Harvard Business School Publishing, 1995), https://hbr.org/1995/05/leading-change-why-transformation-efforts-fail-2, accessed May 2019

18. Malcolm Gladwell, *The Tipping Point* (London: Abacus, 2001)

19. Christian Schwarz, *Natural Church Development* (BCGA & The Drumond Trust, 1998) p. 26.

20. http://www.thebroadcastnetwork.org/episode111 & http://www.thebroadcastnetwork.org/episode112

21. Robert J Karris, *Eating Your Way Through Luke's Gospel* (Collegeville, MN: Liturgical Press, 2006) p. 13.

22. NT Wright, *Jesus and the Victory of God* (London: SPCK, 1996) p. 431.

23. Henri Nouwen, *Reaching Out* (London: HarperCollins, 1990) p. 43.

24. Nelson Searcy, *Maximise: How To Develop Extravagant Givers In Your Church* (Ada, MI: Baker Books, 2010) p. 50.

26. Tony Hsieh, *Delivering Happiness* (London: Business Plus, 2010), p. 175.

28. https://thinktheology.co.uk/blog/article/does_gods_presence_go_missing

31. https://vimeo.com/53658214

33. John C. Maxwell, *Developing the Leaders Around You* (Nashville, TN: Thomas Nelson, 2006) p. 17.

34. Bill Easum, *Leadership on the Other Side* (Nashville, TN: Abingdon Press, 2000) p. 17.

36. Bob Roberts, *The Multiplying Church* (Grand Rapids, MI: Zondervan, 2008) p. 36.

37. L. David Marquet, *Turn the Ship Around! A True Story of Turning Followers into Leaders* (London: Portfolio Penguin, 2013)

38. Craig Groeschel, 'IT: How Leaders Can Get It and Keep It' [message delivered at Willow Creek Leadership Summit 2008]. Referred to in: https://churchm.ag/craig-groeschel-to-reach-people-that-no-one-is-reaching-you-have-to-do-things-that-no-one-is-doing/.

39. Dave Ferguson and Jon Ferguson, *Exponential: How You and Your Friends Can Start a Missional Church Movement* (Grand Rapids, MI: Zondervan, 2010) p. 21.

40. The Tony Robbins Podcast, 'How to innovate in zeros', 25 April 2018. Available at: https://tonyrobbins.libsyn.com/how-to-innovate-in-zeros-jonas-kjellberg-on-how-skype-eliminated-costs-and-took-the-company-to-a-26b-exit-in-just-two-years

41. Simon Sinek, 'How Great Leaders Inspire Action', TEDx Puget Sound, September 2009. Available at: https://www.ted.com/talks/simon_sinek_how_great_leaders_inspire_action

42. Ruth Tucker, *From Jerusalem to Irian Jaya* (Grand Rapids, MI: Zondervan, 2004) p.186.

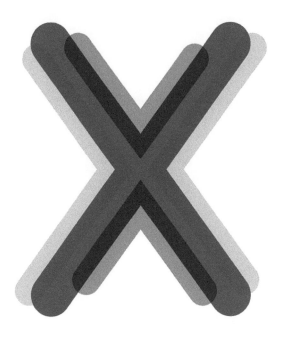

For up-coming events,
online training and coaching,
please go to:

www.multiplanting.com